D1356746

THE
LITTLE
BOOK
OF
LIMERICK

SHARON SLATER

ILLUSTRATED BY GARY O'DONNELL

The History Press Ireland

Dedicated to the memory of
Eugene Coffey

Central Library, Henry Street,
An Lárleabharlann, Sráid Annraoi
Tel: 8734333

First published 2013

The History Press Ireland
50 City Quay
Dublin 2
Ireland
www.thehistorypress.ie

© Sharon Slater, 2013
Illustrations © Gary O'Donnell

The right of Sharon Slater to be identified as the Author
of this work has been asserted in accordance with the
Copyrights, Designs and Patents Act 1988.

All rights reserved. No part of this book may be reprinted
or reproduced or utilised in any form or by any electronic,
mechanical or other means, now known or hereafter invented,
including photocopying and recording, or in any information
storage or retrieval system, without the permission in writing
from the Publishers.

British Library Cataloguing in Publication Data.
A catalogue record for this book is available from the British Library.

ISBN 978 1 84588 793 3

Typesetting and origination by The History Press

CONTENTS

INTRODUCTION

In a book on Limerick's history you would expect to find tales of the castle, the siege and the Treaty Stone. While these are indeed among the most monumental moments in Limerick's history, they are not the focus of *The Little Book of Limerick*. This book endeavours to bring you the story of the everyday man on the street and the little-known facts of history that could so easily have been forgotten.

That being said, it would be an injustice not to mention the Vikings, the castle and the Treaty Stone, all of which left a huge mark on Limerick society.

The name Limerick dates from at least AD 561 and from then onward there has been a settlement on the Shannon in the area now known as Kings Island from that date. In the early ninth century the Vikings arrived in Limerick after journeying up the Shannon, and upon landing they decided to stay. There are some areas of note to the Vikings still known today in the city, such as the Lax Weir, Lax being the Norse word for Salmon. The site on which St Mary's Cathedral stands today was once a Viking meeting place and the centre for government in the early medieval Viking city.

The Vikings would be overpowered by the Dál gCais in the tenth century, who led his people out of Limerick. It is thought that many moved to the Park area in Corbally, where they became known as the Park Danes. In the mid-eleventh century Limerick was burned to the ground twice in repeated raids on the city.

The Normans arrived to the area in 1173, in a bid to oust the last King of Limerick, Domnall Mór O'Brien. Domnall had built St Mary's Cathedral in 1168, making it one of the oldest buildings in the country in continued use for its original purpose. After his death in 1195 the Normans finally succeeded in capturing the city.

In 1197 Limerick received a charter from King John, which granted the citizens of the city the same rights as the citizens of Dublin city. They were now allowed to elect a mayor and bailiffs who would govern and administer the city. During the first decade of the thirteenth century, Limerick Castle, one of city's most famous landmarks, was planned and built. The castle was a five-sided structure which may have been surrounded by a moat before the construction of the first Thomond Bridge. It was officially named King John's Castle, after the reigning monarch, but has also been known as Limerick Castle throughout its 800 years. The castle housed the city mint, where the currency of the city was pressed.

The castle suffered extensive damage during the sieges of the seventeenth century – probably the most well-known event in Limerick's history. In 1690, after the Jacobites' defeat in the Boyne, they retreated to the walled city of Limerick where they held their own in 1690 while being continually attacked by the Williamite army. In 1691, after the harsh winter, the Williamites returned stronger than before and finally defeated the Jacobites, forcing them from the city and causing William Sarsfield to sign the Treaty of Limerick on the famed Treaty Stone.

The Treaty Stone is believed to mark the spot where the broken Limerick Treaty was signed. However, this is unlikely to be true and the treaty was more likely signed at a table in a nearby tent.

There were actually two treaties signed on 3 October 1691.

The first contained twenty-nine articles dealing with the disbandment of the Jacobite army. The Jaobites were given three options. First, they could leave with their arms and flags and head for France, to continue serving under James II in the Irish Brigade. About 14,000 Jacobites soldiers chose this option and marched to Cork where they sailed to France, many accompanied by their wives and children. The soldiers who left to join the French armies were later referred to as the Flight of the Wild Geese. Second, the soldiers could choose to join the Williamite army. Approximately 1,000 soldiers went with this option. Finally the soldiers had an option of returning to their homes, which about 2,000 of them did.

The second treaty signed that day, which would become known as the Broken Treaty, contained thirteen articles dealing with the rights of the defeated Jacobite landed gentry. The majority of the Jacobite gentry who remained in Ireland were Catholics. Under the terms of the treaty their property was not to be confiscated so long as they swore allegiance to William and Mary. Starting in 1695, a series of harsh penal laws were enacted by the Irish parliament to make it difficult for the Irish Catholic gentry who had not taken the oath by 1695 to remain Catholic.

Between 1703 and 1724 'Roman Catholic Strangers', or those who were not native to the city, were banned from living within the walls of Limerick.

In 1791 a military barracks was built within the castle and a hundred members of the British army as well as their families lived here until 1922. During this time it was known as the Castle Barracks.

In 1935 Limerick Corporation removed part of the castle walls and erected twenty-two houses in the castle yard. These were later demolished in 1989 and King John's Castle was restored as a tourist attraction. In 2013 it was reopened after a year of extensive redevelopment.

But *The Little Book of Limerick* is not about these stories. It does not contain the information that you can find in any tour guide. It is instead an outline of captivating, obscure, amusing and even bizarre facts about Limerick and the people who have lived and visited here throughout the ages. You will find tales on the most extraordinary crimes and punishments, eccentric inhabitants, peculiar traditions as well as some of the most well-known and hidden places. By the time you are finished reading this book you will know something new about the people, the customs and the heritage of this ancient city.

1

DID YOU KNOW?

Did you know that in 1574 Limerick was described by a Spanish Ambassador as, 'stronger and more beautiful than all the other cities of Ireland, well walled with stout walls of hewn marble'? Below is a collection of more 'did you knows', each of which offers an impressive, curious, intriguing, shocking or amusing anecdote of a moment in time of Limerick's history. You may have come across some already, but others will leave you puzzled and in search of further information.

PEOPLE

In 1373 the Mayor of Limerick was Nicholas Blackadder and in 1504 the Sheriff was Nicholas Lawless.

In 1841 there were: seven girls married at thirteen years old, seven girls married at fourteen years old, twenty girls married at fifteen years old and one boy married at fifteen years old.

Bruce's Bank was located at 6 Rutland Street. Bruce only had one leg and the other was an iron stump. To help himself get around he used a blackthorn cane. Whenever a defaulter came begging him for clemency for an overdue loan he would pull out his iron stump and whack it with the blackthorn exclaiming, 'This is the softest part of me!'

Leabharlanna Poibli Chathair Bhaile Átha Cliath
Dublin City Public Libraries

The first Mayoress of Dublin and founding member of Cumann na mBan was Limerick-born Kathleen Clarke (*née* Daly). Kathleen passed away on 29 September 1972, at the age of ninety-four. She was the widow of Thomas S. Clarke, who was executed in Dublin, 3 May 1916.

At the height of his fame as a writer in the 1830s, Gerald Griffin (1803–1840), author of *The Collegians*, which was based on the Colleen Bawn's story, burned all his manuscripts and joined the Christian Brothers.

At least 189,429 Limerick residences emigrated from Ireland between 1851 and 1911, many of whom left for America, Australia and England. The population of Limerick in 2006 was 184,055.

George Geary Bennis, a Limerick man who once had a cafe opposite Cruises Hotel, had no interest in shop keeping and left Limerick for Paris in 1822. There he became an editor for *Galignani* (*The Times of Paris*). In 1848 he saved the life of King Louis Phillipe in a street fracas for which he was awarded the title of 'Chevalier'. When he died in 1866 he bequeath his large collection of books to the people of Limerick.

John Ferrar founded the *Limerick Chronicle* in 1768, which is the oldest continuously run newspaper in Ireland. The playwright John O'Keefe is quoted as saying that John was 'very deaf, yet had a cheerful, animated countenance, thin and of middle size'.

The baptistery of St Mary's Cathedral is the burial place of Catherine Plunkett, who died in 1752. Her husband, Walter, was commissioner of the Limerick mint in 1689.

Joseph Fisher Bennis (1839–1928) and his brother had a shop at 26 Patrick Street, which they later moved to George's Street. The brothers had a keen interest in phrenology and were given permission by the governor of the city gaol to examine some of the heads of the prisoners. One evening in 1860, after closing their shop, the two brothers walked the 15 miles to Quin Abbey and filled a sack each with skulls and walked back to Limerick with the sacks on their backs. Bennis put these skulls on display for the next fifty years. Interestingly, it was the Bennis brothers who first mass imported bananas to Limerick.

In June 1688, on the official birthday of the Prince of Wales, the Mayor of Limerick, Robert Hannah, gave three hogshead of wine to the populace.

Limerick-born Sir Thomas Myles, CB (20 April 1857– 14 July 1937) was president of the Royal College of Surgeons in Ireland. In 1914, he was recruited by James Creed Meredith to help in the importation of guns for the Irish Volunteers.

Thomas Blake (1894–1921), a member of the Irish Volunteers, was shot and killed on St Alphonsus Street. He worked in Laird's Pharmacy on the main strip of O'Connell Street, where his knowledge of chemistry was put to use in the manufacture of munitions and explosives used during the Irish War of Independence.

PLACES

Rutland Street derives its name from Charles Manners (1754-1787), the Fourth Duke of Rutland. He was appointed Lord Lieutenant of Ireland in 1784 and visited Limerick in 1785.

In the terms of the 500-year lease for what would become the People's Park, the Earl of Limerick stipulated that no political or religious meetings would be allowed in the park and no bands would be allowed to play on Sundays.

The recesses of the foundation stone of the Carnegie Building, now the Limerick Art Gallery, contain four bottles. Each of these bottles contain the currency of the day (1903) as well as a copy of the *Limerick Leader*, *Limerick Echo*, *Limerick Chronicle*, *Munster News* and a parchment recording the event.

In 1911 Limerick there were three Barrack Lanes as well as a Barrack Hill, two Church Streets, two New Roads, a New Street and New Walk, a Hall's Range, Hall's Lane and Hall's Bow.

Clare Street was built in the swamp lands originally known as Móin na Muice (the moor of the pigs). James O'Sullivan, a tobacconist who constructed the street, dedicated it in spite to the infamous John FitzGibbon, First Earl of Clare, a staunch anti-Catholic.

The first residents of No. 1 Arthur's Quay were Francis Arthur and his wife Ellen Barrett.

The Park Canal was constructed between 1757 and 1758 to transport goods to and from Limerick City. The canal system was invaluable in the transport of heavy goods, such as turf, potatoes, coal etc. By 1929, with modernisation of transport and the building of the hydroelectric plant at Ardnacrusha, the canal became obsolete and fell into dilapidation. The last barge on the canal was transporting Guinness in 1960.

In 1224, in a royal valuation of King John's Castle, it was found that the goods within it were 'scarcely worth 18 pence'.

On the 21 November 1813, a house in May's Lane, Thomondgate blew up when the occupants were trying to dry gunpowder in an iron pot over an open fire.

BUSINESS/TRADES

In the 1840s there was an extensively high demand for guano (bat droppings) as fertiliser in Limerick.

One of the last coppersmiths in Limerick was called John Heffernan and he conducted his business opposite the city courthouse in the Merchants' Quay. Once when the court was in sitting, Judge Ball sent word that he could not hear witnesses over the sound of the copper hammering. Heffernan sent back the message, 'Tell the judge that he gets paid for talking and I get paid for hammering'. He did eventually shut down works for two days, after which he sent the judge a bill for lost earnings.

In 1787, merchant Philip Roche set out to develop the area that is called Roches Street today. Due to the Penal laws of the time, he was not permitted to buy land as he was a Catholic. He managed to purchase the sites needed using the name of his friend, Dr Pery, who was the Church of Ireland Bishop of Limerick.

The United London Gas Company was contracted to bring light to the city in 1824. Public lighting was not new to Limerick though as the first street lamps were erected in 1696 by Thomas Rose.

Between 1824 and 1870 there were fifty-three straw hat makers recorded in Limerick city, all women.

Between 1769 and 1900 there were twenty-five gun-makers in the city, including one woman, Mary Meel, who operated out of Mary Street in 1788.

In 1957 Limerick had an umbrella factory on Catherine Street. It was owned by a C. Holland.

In 1796 there were 171 recorded flax growers in Limerick. Flax was used for both food and clothing.

In 1906, Number 1 in the telephone exchange belonged to McMahon, Day & Co. Apothecaries on 136 George Street (now O'Connell Street). In 1911 Limerick had two telephone operators, both women, one telephone worker, one telephone wireman and two national telephone inspectors.

Clay pipes were produced in the nineteenth century in Merrit's factory on Broad Street Limerick. Twice a year 50 tons of clay would be imported from Liverpool for the process.

WEATHER

William Wordsworth remarked on the Limerick weather when he visited here in 1829, saying, 'it is raining hard now, and has done so all day'.

From the 3 November 1683 to 9 February 1684 there was a severe frost which caused ice up to 7 or 8 feet thick on the Shannon. Carriages and cattle frequently crossed the river from Kings Island to Parteen, Co. Clare on the ice.

On 6 December 1705 a storm, which lasted from 10 p.m. until 8 a.m. the following morning, ravaged the city. The tide covered half of Thomond Bridge and forced up part of Baal's Bridge. In the St Francis' Abbey, several people trying to save their possessions were drowned. A West Indian vessel laden with indigo and tobacco was driven a considerable distance on land.

The summer of 1723 was so warm and dry that the fruit trees produced fruit twice.

The year 1739 was known as 'The Year of the Great Frost', which lasted forty days. It caused some to survive on 'cats, dogs, mice, carrion, putrid meat, nettles and docking'.

On 4 February 1775 a high tide hit Baal's Bridge and caused several of the houses built on the bridge to collapse.

During the dry summer of 1775 the Abbey River was so low that boys could wade in and pick up the eel, flat fish and salmon peel out of the bed of the river.

On 23 January 1814 the Abbey River was completely frozen over.

The longest absolute drought recoded in Ireland was in Limerick between 3 April and 10 May 1938.

On 5 October 1851, at 5.50 p.m., a tornado ripped through Limerick City. Although it only lasted a few minutes, it caused extensive damage between St John's Hospital and Sarsfiled Bridge.

BUILDINGS/STRUCTURES

St Mary's Cathedral has the only complete set of misericords (mercy seats) left in Ireland. They date from the fifteenth century.

The Augustinian Church, on O'Connell Street in Limerick, is built on the site of an old theatre which the Augustinians bought for just £400 in 1822. By contrast, the original theatre cost the public £5,000 to build.

The fountain in front of St John's Cathedral was erected in 1865. Iron goblets were attached to two spouts to enable the public to drink and fill small containers, while larger containers were filled at the other two spouts.

Over the course of one night in February 1867 a hole appeared in the wall of the barracks on the Wolfe Tone Street side. The hole was 12 feet wide and how it was created was unknown as there was no disturbance during the night, only a surprise discovery in the morning.

St John's Hospital began as a three-bed ward in the old St John's Barracks at the personal expense of Lady

Lucy Hartstonge in 1781. Lucy was the wife of Henry Hartstonge of Hartstonge Street and Sir Harry's Mall.

The Dock Clock, which was the guide to all the dockworkers, was designed by harbour engineer William J. Hall and was erected in 1880.

The A1 Bar on Clare Street in Limerick was once an RIC (Royal Irish Constabulary) Police Barracks. The RIC were based here to combat 'night maunders' but after a few months with no incidences the constables were moved into Irishtown.

EDUCATION

The Good Shepherd Convent on Clare Street, which is now the Limerick Institute of Technology Art College, was originally located on the site of an old Lancastrian School, founded around 1806. The school system was developed by Joseph Lancaster for the education of the poor in the early nineteenth century. His system was to employ the more advanced boys as monitors, or assistant teachers, in an effort to enable a few masters to teach a large number of boys. Spelling and reading were taught from charts hung on the walls, thereby dispensing with the need for books for the poor and slates were used to write on, to save paper.

In 1902, in the Limerick Free Library, there were 5,199 volumes comprising: theological, 105; travel, 227; history and biography, 1,615; economics, 135; science, 612; arts, 79; poetry, 159; fiction, 1,739; miscellaneous, 528.

ADVERTISEMENTS

An advert from 1812 reads:

> I caution the Master Coopers of Ireland against employing Edmond Ryan, my indentured apprentice, who eloped from me (two years of his servitude being unexpired) as I am determined, upon his apprehension, to prosecute him according to the law, as well as those who have harboured or employed him. – George Hickey – An Apprentice wanted – One who can procure good bail and is determined to be no Night Walker.

An advert from 1840 reads:

> A Lady wishes to procure a situation for a highly respectable, trustworthy, and good-tempered middle-aged Woman, who has been many years in service and would be particularly well suited to act as attendant on an Elderly Lady, or an Invalid.

An advert from 1852 reads:

> St John's Fever Hospital. The Governors of the above Institution are desirous of contracting for the supplies of the undermentioned articles, to be delivered at the Hospital as may be required, from time to time to first of May next –

> Best White Bread, per 12oz, bricks.
> Best New Milk per gallon.
> Good fresh killed beef, 1st and 2d rounds.
> Mutton, per lb.
> Best Irish Yellow Soap per cwt.
> Best Mould and Dipt Candles per lb.
> Good dry Outen Straw per Ton.
> Good dry Turf per Kish.

Groceries.

Whiskey per gallon.

Port Wine per bottle.

Leeches and Medicine, per list, to be seen at the Hospital.

Sealed tenders will be received by the Committee at the Parish Commissioners Offices, Upper Cecil Street, up to 3 o'clock on Monday, the 25th inst. The committee will not be bound to accept the lowest tender.

An advert from 1885 reads:

Wanted at once, a strong, respectable, county girl; must be first-class butter maker and milker; must understand thoroughly the rearing of calves and poultry, and be willing to make herself generally useful.

TRAGEDY

The ship *Kapunda* sailed on 11 December 1887 from London for Freemantle, Western Australia. It never reached its destination, having been run down and sunk by an unknown vessel. All 300 passengers were lost including Limerick citizens, Michael Bolans, his wife and four children and John Buckley, twenty-two, a farm labourer.

In a shocking accident on the 12 February 1693, one of the towers which defended the entrance of the quay fell down. It contained 250 barrels of gunpowder which were blown up by the collapse. The Sheriff, Mr Bowman, the Councillor, John Lacy, one Mr Lillis, along with 200 members of the public were killed or mangled. The explosion literally shook the entire town and some people reportedly were killed by stones thrown up to a mile away from the accident. The impact was felt as far away as Kilmallock.

2

BUILDINGS

Without the buildings there would be no city and if the walls could talk we would hear many tales of happiness and woe. Here are some of the buildings in Limerick City and a small fragment of their history.

THE HOUSE WITH 100 YEARS OF HISTORY

The house at 22 Cecil Street Upper has been witness to over 100 years of history. The plot of land on which it stands was first leased by Pryce Peacock in 1809. The house, unlike many others on the street, was a smaller late Georgian house, which was most likely built sometime in the 1830s. It contained eight inhabitable rooms and in 1911 had two outhouses, or turf houses, and an external drop for coal. The house that stood at 22 Upper Cecil Street in the Shannon Ward held many families, many tales and doubtless many secrets.

1840–1850
One of the first occupiers of the house was Robert Ringrose Gelston, who moved there in 1840. Mr Gelston came to Limerick in 1838, at the age of 23, to set up practice as a surgeon after studying in Glasgow. He quickly settled into his new home and integrated himself into Limerick

society, so much so that he was elected joint High Sherriff of Limerick in 1841. Later, in 1842, he served the position solely. In April 1845 he voluntarily served in the local Workhouse hospital, as the minutes show that, 'Robert R. Gelstan Esq. be and is hereby elected Assistant Surgeon to this institution to act without salary.'

In late 1845 he married Miss Elizabeth Philips of Guile of Tipperary, turning the house into a family home. The couple had at least two children who were baptised in St Michael's Church of Ireland. Additionally, Robert is mentioned in the Church of Ireland Financial Report of the Diocesan Council of the Diocese of Limerick for the year ending 31 December 1882.

The family moved to 68 George Street before 1859, where Robert spent the rest of his life. In 1893 his eyesight began to fail and he retired from professional life. He passed away on 11 February 1908 in 68 George Street at the age of ninety-three and was buried in St Munchin's Graveyard.

Another interesting thing that occurred at this residence was on 3 September 1848, when Mr Hampton, Mr Hampden Russell and Mr Townsend made a successful ascent in a hot-air balloon, *Erin-Go-Bragh*, from the yard in Cecil Street.

1850–1870

Henry Norwell and his wife came to occupy the property in 1850, when the value of the house and lands was recorded as £10 10s. He rented the house from the landlord at the time, Mr Edward Cruise, the owner of the Cruise Hotel. Mrs Norwell passed away at the age of forty-seven while they lived here, as her death was recorded in the *Limerick Chronicle* on the 12 January 1853. Not much else is known about the Norwells, except that Henry died in Belfast in late December 1854.

The next notable tenant was Jonathan Elmes, who moved into the house in 1856. Just like Mr Gelston,

Jonathan was a physician/surgeon. Jonathan was born in Kilbrogan Parish in Bandon, Co. Cork in 1809 to Thomas and Mary Elmes. In June 1835 he qualified as a surgeon. Ten years later, on 8 July, he married Miss Diana Sachville Dunlevie and they had at least one child.

Jonathan contributed a great deal to Limerick society. First, on 17 October 1860, he was one of thirty-two doctors who signed a petition to encourage the corporation to provide public baths in the city, in an effort to aid the health and hygiene of Limerick's citizens. Then, in 1862, he donated £1 to the foundation of the Limerick Athenaeum, a theatre that would be built across the street from 22 Upper Cecil Street.

In 1866 Dr Elmes had a disagreement with one of his servants, Thomas Reidy of Hall's Range. This caused the doctor to take the servant to court but the charges of using violent, threatening and abuse language were later dropped.

Interestingly, there was a time in Jonathan's life when he was mistakenly thought to have died. On 16 July 1885 there was a report in the *Limerick Chronicle* that Jonathan Elmes had died, but in the very next issue of the paper it was revealed that this was an error; that although he had suffered a major illness he did not in fact pass away at that time. After leaving the house on Cecil Street, the family moved to 34 George Street and again to Thomas Street, where Jonathan ultimately passed away on 16 November 1893.

1870–1901

In 1877 there were a number of occupants, including David L. Meany, whose line of work is unknown. David only remained in the building for a short period while the other tenants, John and Patrick Fitzgerald, who both worked as Clerks, remained there from 1877 to 1880. The final tenant from 1877 was John Joyce, who was employed as a pilot. He remained living in the house until at least 1886.

It is unknown who, if anyone, resided in the house during the 1890s. But in 1901 the house was occupied by James Burke, a sixty-six-year-old widowed flour miller, along with his servant Jane Browne and her sister Mary Ellen Browne, who worked as a housemaid but was visiting her sister the night of the census that year.

All three of the occupants were Roman Catholic and could read and write. The Browne sisters were both born in different counties: Jane was born on 13 November 1877 in Limerick and Mary Ellen Browne was born 27 February 1880 in Galway. Their father, William Browne, was a member of the RIC and was posted to Galway, while their mother, Bridget, was a native of Castleconnell in Limerick. William retired on 15 August 1887 to Annacotty in Limerick and he passed away in 1900. After this his widow and their children moved into the city centre. Jane Browne went on to marry Charles Moore, whose father was also in the RIC, on 28 September 1901 in St John's Cathedral. Her sister Mary married a Gerald Flynn.

1902–1940

After 1907 the house was occupied by Margaret Shiels, a forty-three-year-old devoted Roman Catholic, and her family. In 1901 Margaret and her husband John were living at 11 Ellen Street, where Margaret worked as a shopkeeper and John as a plumber. After John passed away on 20 November 1906, after battling tuberculosis for two years, Margaret, her seven children and her sister moved to the house on Cecil Street.

In April 1911, the children still living with her were: Christina (twenty-three) and Mary (eighteen), who both worked as tailors; Peter (seventeen), who had followed in his father's footsteps and become a plumber; Bridget (sixteen) who had followed her mother's example and was a shop assistant; and Ellen (fourteen), Gerard (ten) and Josephine (six), all who were attending school. In 1911 Christina Shiels married Ambrose Shea.

Margaret's sister, Bridget Moloney, a spinster, had been living with the Shiels family since at least 1901, where she was recorded, mistakenly, as John Shiels aunt. The family was still in the house in 1923 when Margaret Shiels, her son Peter and daughter Ellen also known as Lena were recorded as living there.

John Shiels, Margaret's son, enlisted as a Sapper in the Royal Engineers, 12th Field Company and was killed in action during the First World War, on 9 August 1915. His body was never recovered but he is memorialised on the Ypres (Menin Gate) Memorial, Belgium.

In 1911 there were three boarders also living in the house, presumably to help Margaret with the financial costs of supporting eight family members. These boarders were Daniel McAuliffe, a fifty-seven-year-old single Catholic man living on independent means; Michael McNamara, a thirty-four-year-old married stationary engine driver from Limerick; and David Shiels, a fifty-seven-year-old widowed

Presbyterian tin smith from Scotland. It is unknown if David Shiels was related to Margaret's late husband.

Between 1915 and at least 1920 a Mrs Daly ran the house as a series of apartments. In 1916 one of her tenants was John O'Connell, he was one of 273 prisoners who were removed from Richmond Barracks on 12 May 1916 and lodged in Wakefield Detention Barracks on 13 May for his part in the 1916 rising. In 1923, the Shiels family was joined by Joseph, Mary Kevin and Michael Mulqueen.

By 1931, Jeremiah and Ellen Carmody, John and Joseph Enright were sharing the house. Jeremiah continued to live there until at least 1940, this time with a Bridget Carmody.

These are only the bare facts covering the history of one house in Limerick over the course of 100 years; the house next door to this would have had a completely different and varied history of its occupants. If these walls could talk they would speak for days.

THE STATE OF LIMERICK BUILDINGS IN THE 1800s

Limerick in the 1800s was a city divided. On one side there was the Newtown, with its elegant buildings and freshly paved roads, and on the other the Irishtown and Englishtown, where the buildings were falling apart and the sewers overflowed into the streets. The latter area was often overlooked and entirely forgotten by the city council as most of the well-to-do residents, whose voice took priority, moved to the Newtown with its indoor plumbing and clean streets. This left the poor and less fortunate of the city to waste away in squalor.

In the Irishtown area, which included John Street, Broad Street and Mungret Street, the houses were in a general state of decay, some only being held together with props between the lanes. They sported a mishmash of styles and varied in building materials.

The Englishtown area, from Thomond Bridge to Baals Bridge including Mary Street, Nicholas Street, was of the same ilk of Irishtown but had even older structures, including some medieval buildings.

The Newtown area, from Patrick Street to O'Connell Avenue, from the river to Gerald Griffin Street, was built in Georgian style.

A TRAGIC DEATH CAUSED BY BUILDING DETERIORATION

Limerick in the late nineteenth century was an extremely religious place, so it was unsurprising that eighteen-year-old Christina McNamara was a very pious young woman.

Shortly after 8 p.m. one Saturday night, the 18 February 1899, young Christina left her home on John Street to make her way to St Mary's Chapel on Athlunkard Street. She would have been wrapped up warm for the cold winter evening. Keeping with the fashion among the poor of the time, she would have most likely been wearing a long woollen dress, her skirt undoubtedly dragging along the path. Her feet would have been protected with ankle-high boots that fastened with hook buttons and a woollen shawl would have been draped over her head and shoulders.

At the same time that she was making her way to the chapel, the Local Acting Sergeant Doherty was dealing with a group of young boys who had gathered in Broad Street and were causing a ruckus on the path. Doherty shooed the boys home and continued towards Baals Bridge. Little did he know that there would soon be a much larger issue to be dealt with than some rowdy boys. As he reached the bridge he was startled by a loud crash from behind him. He immediately turned around and saw a cloud of dust rising from the footpath in Broad Street.

The sergeant, along with other passers-by, rushed to the scene, to find that part of Mr Shine's three-storey house had collapsed. Bricks were seen falling from the wall and the remaining part of roof, which had large flags on it. Three of the boys, one of whom was Ned Sheehan, who had only just been shooed away, were pulled from the rubble with minor injuries. A middle-aged man, Patrick Minihan of Bowles Lane, and Edward Purtill of John's Square had both received wounds to the head.

As the dust finally began to settle, young Christina was discovered on the ground, partly covered in debris and with a large flagstone crushing down on her legs. The crowd worked together to free the girl and eventually succeeded and quickly carried her to Barrington's Hospital on the other side of Baal's Bridge. The other three injured men were also brought to the hospital and were all tended by Dr McGrath and Nurse Haughton. Christina remained alive, although unconscious, until five o'clock the following morning, when she succumbed to her injuries and passed away. Her family buried her in Mount Saint Lawrence Cemetery on 25 February 1899.

Upon examining the scene of the accident, which was just a portion of a larger house owned by Miss Mary Griffin and being rented by Mr Shine, it was discovered that the house was at least a few hundred years old and seemed, of all the houses in the street, the most likely to collapse. A notice was posted to the occupiers of the house on 20 February, two days after the accident, warning them that the building was in a dangerous state. Mr Shine went on record stating that he did not feel that there was anything wrong with the roof, apart from a leak and as Miss Griffin had replaced the rafters only thirteen years before, he considered it safe.

Many of the houses on the street had used props to support the walls in the small lanes off the main street. It was believed that if these props were removed that the entire house which they supported would certainly collapse. Two years earlier, in February 1897, a similar house on John Street completely collapsed in on itself, but there were no reported injuries or fatalities.

A notice was issued during the inquest into Christina's death stating, 'that in view of the danger to lives of residents and the public generally having business in John Street, Mungret Street and Broad Street and the old town generally, we beg to call attention to owners of property and other responsible officials of the insecure state of the same and their dilapidated condition in said area.'

INJURIES CAUSED BY FAULTY WORKMANSHIP

It was not only old buildings that were a danger in Limerick, new buildings had their own failings as well. The first English Employer's Liability Act was passed in 1880. The original Act was very weak. In fact, it only

provided benefits for seven out of one hundred workers. In 1897, the British legislature proposed new legislation to provide a remedy for the injured worker. The authors of the legislation sought to have injured workers compensated for each industrial accident and to make the economic burden for the compensation system part of the cost of production. The employee was not required to prove negligence on the part of the employer, but rather had to demonstrate that the injury had occurred during the employment situation. The Act was limited to certain occupations which included factory labour, mine and quarry activities and engineering. Neither the original Employers' Liability Act of 1880 nor the Workmen's Compensation Act of 1897, the latter having been intended to encourage greater attention to safety in the industrial environment, was successful in reducing the number of industrial accidents in the British work place.

First Story

John Ryan & Sons builders were contracted to erect a new building at the Magdalene Asylum on Clare Street on 30 August 1895. There were five men working on the scaffolding of this building, setting a large wooden frame used to make an archway, when the scaffolding collapsed beneath them. All five men fell the 35 feet to the ground, which was covered with rough masonry. The wooden planks of the scaffolding then collapsed in on the men. All five named, John McGrath, John Kenny, Michael Dundon, John O'Brien and James Flanagan, suffered horrific injuries and it seemed miraculous that any of them had survived the fall. The only one to succumb to his injuries was John McGrath, a stonemason from Kilrush. His wife and ten children were left to bury him and find a way to survive without him. The accident was found to be caused by one broken plank on the scaffolding. If it had been erected correctly it should have been able to bear a weight of two or three tons.

Second Story

Thirty-six-year-old John Quinlan, who lived on Taylor Street, was a mason working with four others on scaffolding about 35 feet from the ground at the back of Barrington's hospital on 29 April 1896. He was partnered with another mason, William Doherty, a twenty-four-year-old married man from The Abbey. One of the men was on the inside of the wall they were building, while the other was on the outside. John Quinlan went to raise the line of his score of work and after having done so stepped onto the wall to get to the scaffolding on the other side. He put his foot on freshly laid brick, which were not sufficiently set, and it went from under him, sending him 30 feet to the ground below. William Doherty immediately went to help raise Quinlan, who said to him, 'Don't hurt my arms', as one of his shoulders had dislocated. The workmen managed to carry John Quinlan upstairs to a bed where he died later that afternoon.

GOING UNDERGROUND INTO THE SEWERS

The sewers are a very interesting feature of Limerick architecture, below is a description of their foundation and construction. The area concerned is Newtownpery, though it was called South Prior's Land before building work began. The land was marshland and was mainly owned by Edmond Sexton Pery with the Mardyke (Rutland Street area) owned by Patrick Arthur. Newtownpery would stretch from Rutland Street to O'Connell Avenue, from the Shannon up to Gerald Griffin Street in some places. Around 1769, Edmond Sexton Pery enlisted local architect Christopher Colles to survey the pre-existing buildings and to propose the structure of the new city. Colles plan was the grid format that we know today.

The marshy nature of the ground meant that traditional foundations were not possible. This led to the construction of the area in an interesting way, from the cellars up. So the cellars/vaults and tunnels/sewer are actually constructed on original ground level, while the road and main houses are on the first floor and the ground level built up to the correct height. We know that many of these vaults were used as coal bunkers (as evident from the coal chutes lids on street level), also for food storage.

Although several plans survive for the above ground building – the preconstruction map of 1769, Ferrars 1787 map (which was just an updated version of the original plan), the post-construction survey of the Pery Estate by James and Martin Coffey 1823 and Ordnance Survey map of 1840 – no plans survive which show the vaults and sewers. They are, however, mentioned in some of the documentation, for example, the lease agreements for plots in the Arthurs Quay area from 1792, from the Leahy-Arthur Deeds, states that the properties were 'bounded in front by area wall and underneath the street by the termination of the vaults to the house'.

The main sewers ran through the centre of the streets (under-roads) and were flanked by the vaults for the houses on each side. These sewers were originally accessible via the vaults, as plumbing as we know it today did not exist during the time of the buildings construction and so the waste from the house was disposed of manually into these sewers. The sewers themselves were 8 feet high and 3 feet 6 inches wide on the main streets (O'Connell Street, William Street, Thomas Street, Catherine Street ...) while the smaller sewers of the side streets were about 4 feet high by 2 feet 3 inches. These sewers were partly excavated from the rock (in the higher streets) and had vaulted ceilings of stone or brick.

These sewers exited the street into the river and so during high tide they were prone to flooding. As indoor plumbing became popular and to prevent the backwash from high tide, most of the entrances were bricked up, though the sewers themselves remained.

On the night of the 6th or the morning of 7 March 1895 there was a very daring robbery in 19 Rutland Street, Limerick city and the perpetrators used the sewers to gain access. Below is the extract from the *Limerick Leader* from Friday, 8 March 1895:

> The premises of Mr. D Lyons, publican, Rutland Street, which adjoin the old post office, were burglariously entered, and a sum of £7 15s and a quantity of brandy and tea stolen. Entrance was effected apparently in the following manner. It appears that a number of vaults communicate with the river from Rutland Street, the houses having to be built thereon because of the influx of tide. Since the burning of the premises at Matthew Bridge the openings to these vaults are exposed in the fenced plot of ground near the bridge, and it was through one of these passages that the burglars and made their way into Mr Lyons' premises. In order to enter the shop it was necessary that a wall should be broken through, and it is evident, viewing the circumstances surrounding the matter that the perpetrators were well acquainted with the nature of Mr. Lyons business, and the fact that he does not live on the premises. Mr Lyons closed his premises before eleven o'clock on Wednesday night, leaving the cash stated on the premises. When he returned on Thursday morning he missed the money brandy and tea. The police communicated with, and a vigorous search instituted but so far to no avail. The police however do not despair of getting some clue to the perpetrators of the robbery.

Daniel Lyons lived on Wellesley Place, now known as Clontarf Place with his family. He ran the business on Rutland Street from at least 1884 until at least 1901.

3

BRIDGES

Limerick city was founded on an island, later known as Kings Island, and so as the city grew and developed bridges were needed to access the island. The first known of these bridges was Baal's Bridge, built about 1340. This bridge connected the Englishtown on the island to the Irishtown in St John's Parish. The second was over Thomond Bridge to the Thomondgate area. As the city expanded into Corbally and Newtownpery further bridges were added. These bridges were built and rebuilt, named and renamed, but each one holds a history and a story.

BAAL'S BRIDGE

The first Baal's Bridge was constructed about 1340 as the city expanded across the Abbey River to the opposite bank. This bridge had four arches with a range of houses across it.

The name Baal's Bridge, or Droichead Maol (Bald Bridge) as it is known in Irish, could derive from a variety of sources. One possibility is that the name derives from bald, meaning that, originally, the bridge was without parapets. The old bridge was reputed to be owned by the Earl of Shannon, whose family name was Boyle. Hence the bridge could very well have been called 'Boyle's Bridge', corrupted later to 'Baal's Bridge' or 'Ball's Bridge'. Also in the early nineteenth century there was much uninformed speculation that such bridges were called after Baal, a Pagan God, but the name most frequently used is Ball's Bridge.

In 1760 the old town wall, which ran from Quay Lane to Baal's Bridge, was torn down, making way for George's Quay. The houses on the east side of Baal's Bridge were knocked down in 1761, to widen the bridge and allow for two carts to pass.

Some of these houses were occupied by wealthy and successful traders, such as:

The Worrell family, who had a boot and shoemaker's shop there from at least 1788 until 1824
John Cullun, silversmith, 1769
Richard Evans, woollen drapers, 1769
John Hanrahan, boot and shoemakers, 1769
James Walsh, boot and shoemaker, 1788
Thomas O'Donnell, boot and shoemaker, 1788
Michael Kearney, woollen drapers, 1788
Simon Kent, skinner, 1769
William Mausell, merchant, 1769
Patrick MacNemara, skinner, 1769
Michael Neville, whip makers, 1769
Richard Roche, linen draper, 1769
John Russell, linen draper, 1769
Michael Sellors, linen draper, 1824
John Ryan, glover, 1788
Richard Wheeler, hat maker and dealer, 1824

An interesting piece of history concerning one of the houses on Baal's Bridge involved a house owned by Mr Benny. During the high tides of 1775 the floor of Mr Berry's house on the bridge collapsed, taking its owner with it. Mr Berry was carried by the tide to Mathew Bridge where he was rescued by the sailor, John Fitzgerald.

The modern bridge was designed by the Pain Brothers and built in 1831. The Pain Brothers were renowned architects who were responsible for many of the iconic structures in Limerick city's landscape, including Thomond Bridge and Athlunkard Bridge.

The current structure was built between 1830 and 1831 and is a single-arched hump-back limestone bridge. It replaced an earlier four-arched bridge which had stood in the same spot since about 1430 and was also the only link before the mid-eighteenth-century bridge crossing the Abbey River between Englishtown and Irishtown. Early drawings show a row of houses on the bridge before it was replaced, but by the early nineteenth century these houses were beginning to collapse. During the construction of the new bridge in 1830 a significant archaeological object was found in the foundations of the old bridge. A brass Square of Freemasonry symbolism was found in the foundations with an inscription dating from 1507. Also inscribed on the square is the text 'I will strive to live with love and care upon the level, by the square'. It is reputed to be one of the earliest Masonic items to be found in the world.

THOMOND BRIDGE

Thomond Bridge, like many of the other bridges in the city, has gone through a few incarnations to what we see crossing the river today. It is most likely that the first Thomond Bridge would have been erected about 1185 as a lead from King John's Castle to the Clare side of the Shannon. This bridge contained fourteen arches, a toll house and a guard house. The guard house was removed in 1761.

The newer bridge, whose proposal for replacement was made to the Corporation in 1816, wasn't built until 1840 with William Henshaw Owen as resident engineer and the Pain brothers as designers.

Thomond Bridge and the Bard of Thomond, Michael Hogan's poem 'The Bishops Lady and the Drunked Thady' go hand in hand in Limerick folklore. The story goes that the wife of the bishop, who resided in Bishop's Palace on Church Street just off Thomond Bridge, was not a lady of virtue. She was said to have enjoyed all the vices of the living. Her death came all too soon for the Lady but her hell was to remain close to her old stomping ground between Thomond

Bridge and Castle Street. This is where she would roam nightly terrorising passers-by. Now enters the drunkard Thady into the story, who had a wholesome fear of ever meeting the lady. Thady was a learned man, well respected by all but he was too fond of his tipple. So came the eventful night when Thady was caught up in a fight, as the guards were sent for he set off in a scurry forgetting for a moment about our lady on the bridge. Remembering after he passed the first of the fourteen arches of the old bridge he thought himself lucky to have escape her that night. 'When lo' just as his fears had left him then the lady appeared and grabbed him.

She had a ferocious temper and the strength that comes with a strong will, soon she had Thady in the air and over the wall. Down he came with a splash into the roaring Shannon River which carried him down stream. He soon sobered up and decided that the river in which he learned to swim would not become his grave that night. He spotted the anchor of a nearby boat and pulled himself to safety. He was found on the shore in the morning and swore off the drink, he devoted the rest of his life to serving God, and his neighbour through honest hard labour

Legend has it that you can see the fingerprints of those who were gripping to the bridge for dear life after being thrown by the Bishop's Lady to this day, which would be a feat in itself as the bridge haunted by the Bishop's lady was replaced in 1840.

MATHEW BRIDGE

Prior to the modern structure of Mathew Bridge, there was a previous bridge on this site known simply as New Bridge, which was built when the West Watergate was demolished in 1761. This demolition caused Assembly Mall, now known as Charlottes Quay, to be formed, in which houses built by the Russell and Vokes families take up prized positions.

In 1840 the last tie to the New Bridge was broken with the death of Timothy Donovan at 102 years old. It was said that he laid the first stone in the New Bridge.

The bridge we see today is Mathew Bridge, which was completed in June 1846 under the supervision of contractor, John Duggan. It was financed by the Corporation and the City and County Grand Juries. It was named after Fr. Theobald Mathew, a friar who launched a national temperance movement. In 1846 it is said that he had obtained 180,000 disciples in Limerick, at the time the population of Limerick city and county was about 250,000. The bridge was constructed during the mayorship of William I Geary MD.

On this bridge there was a small jewellers shop; folklore tells us that during the great famine of the 1840s one man down on his luck, on hearing that prisoners were being transported for committing crimes, hatched a plan. He walked to the jewellers and smashed the window, placing his hands upon the jewels and waited to be arrested. How true this story is has not been ascertained but it speaks volumes of the desperation of the time. There were other cases throughout the city where men and women stole and stood to find a better life beyond these shores.

SARSFIELD BRIDGE

Sarsfield Bridge is the second of Limerick's River Shannon crossings, the first being Thomond Bridge. The bridge was needed to create a quicker route from the newly developed Newtownpery to the large houses on the North Strand (Clancy's Strand).

The foundation stone was laid on 25 October 1824 and the bridge, which was designed by Alexander Nimmo and cost £89,061, was opened 5 August 1835. The bridge entered the city into what was known as Brunswick Street, now Sarsfield Street. The bridge was originally known as the Wellesley Bridge after Marquess Richard Wellesley (1760-1842), a Lord Lieutenant of Ireland. Wellesley lived for many years with a French actress Hyacinth-Gabrielle Roland and they had five children together before they married.

A section of the bridge on the Sarsfield Street side had a swivel action that could open to allow large vessels to pass into the upper quays, such as Arthur's quay. While this function is no longer in use, the mechanisms can still be seen under the bridge. Between 1907 and 1910 the swivel access was only opened to allow seventy-seven boats through. The swivel bridge was last opened in the 1923.

It was a toll bridge from 1835 until 1883. The abolition of the toll has been commemorated by a plaque on the bridge which reads:

Sarsfield Bridge by authority of Parliament and through liberal grants from the Grand Juries of Limerick and Clare Alderman Jerome Counihan J.P. Mayor of Limerick 1882–1883 was enabled to declare this bridge free of toll on Easter Monday 26 March 1883 William Boyd J.P. High Sheriff Alfred G. Wallace Sol. Town Clerk.

Following the abolition of the tolls, the remaining debt on the Wellesley Bridge was transferred to the Grand Jury of Limerick and the Grand Jury of Clare. Limerick Corporation took over the maintenance and lighting of the bridge, and the Limerick Harbour Commissioners were charged with manning the swivel bridge and approaches.

The bridge was renamed Sarsfield to commemorate Patrick Sarsfield, the Earl of Lucan, who is renowned in Limerick for his role in the Williamite War and the 1691 siege, and the Treaty of Limerick in particular.

On the left side of the bridge as you leave the city there is a monument which commemorates the 1916 rising, located on the bridge just above the Limerick Rowing Club building. This statue replaced an earlier one of Viscount

Fitzgibbon, which was flanked by two Russian cannons captured in the Crimean War. Viscount Fitzgibbon, was killed in the Charge of the Light Brigade at Balaclava in 1854. This statue was blown up by the Irish Republican Army in 1930.

Off the bridge is a manmade island, originally called Wellesley Pier, but which is now known as Shannon Island. Rowing clubhouses sit on Shannon Island at either side of the bridge. The Shannon Rowing Club to the right as you leave the city was founded by Sir Peter Tait in 1868. Two years later, in 1870, the Limerick Rowing Club was established.

THE SYLVESTER O'HALLORAN FOOTBRIDGE

This footbridge, built in 1987, crosses the Abbey River from the Potato Market to behind the Hunt Museum. Hundreds of people cross this small pedestrian bridge on a monthly basis, some having left their cars in the Potato Market, others after visiting City Hall or St Mary's Cathedral, while a few will use it to escape the hustle and pollution on Mathew Bridge. Standing on this foot bridge, facing the Shannon they are met with the majestic view of this magnificent river, a fitting place indeed for a memorial bridge in honour of Limerick man Dr Sylvester O'Halloran.

Dr Sylvester O'Halloran was born in Caherdavin on 31 December 1728 to strong patriotic Catholic parents, Michael O'Halloran and Mary McDonnell. His brother, Father Joseph Ignatius O'Halloran (1718–1800), was a Jesuit priest and professor of philosophy at the University of Bordeaux.

After studying in Limerick with his mother's cousin, Seán Clárach Mac Domhnaill, a Gaelic poet, Sylvester considered a career in the priesthood but, touched by those he saw afflicted by premature blindness and lack of medical personnel in Limerick, he determined to become a surgeon and was educated in London, Leyden and Paris (at the time his Catholic faith made it virtually impossible for him to take up his studies in Dublin).

His passionate commitment to education, research and surgical skills marked him out from his contemporaries. He went on to develop a new, ground-breaking method of treating cataracts and in 1750 published his work in *A New Treatise on Glaucoma, or Cataract in Ireland*. He also published the valuable *New Method of Amputation* in 1765.

Sylvester O'Halloran never turned his back on his native city of Limerick and he gave many years to St John's Hospital. In 1773, along with Dr Patrick Unthank, he established a lie-in hospital for pregnant women, to which he gave his time for free. He was one of the founders of the Limerick County Infirmary on Mulgrave Street, which unfortunately wasn't completed until four years after his death. The hospital's foundation stone is now preserved in the Sylvester O'Halloran Post Graduate Centre at the Mid-Western Regional Hospital in Limerick.

O'Halloran had been very impressed while in France with the Académie Royale de Chirurgie, which had been founded in Paris in 1731. Sylvester O'Halloran's *Proposals for the Advancement of Surgery in Ireland* and his driving enthusiasm were directly responsible for the establishment of the Royal College of Surgeons in Ireland in 1784. An annual meeting was established in 1992 by Peter Delaney called the Sylvester O'Halloran Meeting and is held at the Royal College of Surgeons in his honour.

Not only was he a master surgeon, but he was also an avid historian and patriot, writing *A History of Ireland* in 1774. This book, however, was not published until 1804, and was met with disdain from those who believed the details it contained on the Anglo-Irish ascendancy should have remained unrecorded.

He married Mary O'Casey and had five children only one of whom, Joseph, survived him. He died in his house near St Mary's Cathedral on 11 August 1807 and was subsequently buried in his family vault in Killeely graveyard.

The inscription on his headstone reads, 'His country's honours and good name ever found him a ready and unflinching champion. Erected by the St Senan's Historical Society.'

THE ABBEY BRIDGE

The Abbey Bridge is the most recently built bridge in Limerick. It was officially opened, with some controversy, in 1999. The initial plan was to name the bridge the Jim Kemmy Bridge, after the former mayor and local historian who passed away in 1997. Local residents disagreed with this name and called for the bridge to be named the Abbey Bridge after the Abbey Fishermen families who lived in the area for generations. After much deliberation the name change was agreed upon and the bridge stands in honour of the Abbey Fisherman. Jim Kemmy was honoured with a more fitting memorial as the new name for the city museum, The Jim Kemmy Memorial Museum.

The Abbey fishermen consisted primarily of four families; Clancy, McNamara, Shanny and Hayes. Three of these four families lived in the Abbey area of Limerick city; the fourth, the Shannys, lived in an area just outside the city called Park. All the men would frequent 'Shannys Pub', a pub on the Shannon River near to the Blackbridge run by three Shanny sisters. This pub opened onto the river so the men could enter straight from here.

Other names that have been associated with the Abbey Fishermen were Cherry, O'Dwyer, Lyddy, Hartigan, O'Connor and Carroll, but these families were not to stand the test of time on the fisheries.

ATHLUNKARD BRIDGE

The name Athlunkard comes from the Irish 'Áth an Longphuirt', meaning the ford of the fortress or encampment. Athlunkard Bridge, built between 1826 and 1830, is situated on the Corbally Road out of the city.

Designed and built by the famous brothers James and George Richard Pain, this five-arched granite bridge is of high design quality and displays the best stone masonry skills of the day. The bridge cost a total of £7,000 to construct and originally had a tollgate on the city side but, on 28 April 1884, it was declared free of toll.

Three plaques give the dates of the commencement (1826) and completion of the bridge (1830); the name of the architects, the local MP (Thomas Spring Rice); and the county boundary marker.

OTHER LIMERICK BRIDGES

O'Dwyer's Bridge, Athlunkard Street was constructed in 1824 and this lead to the construction of the Park Bridge in 1835, linking the city of Limerick to Corbally. The bridge, which still stands today, was constructed and dedicated to Dr E.T. O'Dwyer, who was consecrated Bishop of Limerick on 29 June 1886. Upon the bridge is a bronze plaque which reads:

This bridge is dedicated to the memory of the Most Revd Dr E.T. O'Dwyer Bishop of Limerick (1886-1917) an honorary Freeman of the City in recognition of his great services to Church and Country A.D. 1931. Alderman Patrick Donnellan Mayor, J.J. Roughan Engineer, J.J. Peacocke City Surveyor, William M. Nolan Town Clerk.

Shannon Bridge is known as the Whistling, Whining or Singing Bridge, as after construction wind would blow though the gaps under the bridge making a whistling sound. While true after its original construction, this architectural default has now been remedied. It was opened on 30 May 1988 and to this day is still the last bridge that crosses the Shannon River.

The Canal Bridge was designed by Dutch architect Uzuld, who also designed the Lock Mill. This quaint redbrick and limestone bridge was erected in 1757 to cross the newly created canal. The bridge was once used by horses but is now the reserve of pedestrians and cyclists. The bridge bollards were made by Harrison Lee & Sons, ironmongers, who operated out of Mungret Street and High Street from the 1840s into the twentieth century.

The Park Road Bridge links Corbally and Rhebogue. It was once a steeper humped bridge, to allow boats to pass beneath it, but has since been lowered. The previous arc is still visible in the internal stone work. This bridge marks the old border of Limerick city and county.

The Guinness Bridge, built in 1996, is a white metal pedestrian bridge on the Canal Bank. As with the Abbey Bridge there was much debate at the time over whether it should be named after another local historian, Kevin Hannan, who passed away earlier that year. It was settled that the bridge would be named after Guinness since in the 1880s, Guinness began sending their porter to Limerick by canal, undercutting the local breweries in the area.

4

BACON
FACTORIES

Limerick is famed for its bacon production. It is said in Limerick that 'everything but the squeak was used' when producing bacon in the factories. Although the vast majority of the pigs were imported from the local environs, many of the city households also kept pigs – along with the more traditional chickens. These pigs were usually fed on domestic scraps as well as on root crops and fattened for the family themselves. Thousands of pigs were slaughtered and processed weekly in the Limerick Bacon factories, which, in the height of their production, were the most consumed pork products in the British Isles. In the nineteenth century Limerick hams became renowned throughout the British Empire with Queen Victoria insisting on Limerick hams at her Christmas dinner. Limerick pork, through the O'Mara's factory, was even exporting as far away as Russia and Romania in 1891 and 1902 respectively.

The four great bacon factories in Limerick were Matterson's, Shaw's, O'Mara's and Denny's, each competing for local, national and international trade out of Limerick City during the nineteenth and early twentieth century. Other bacon merchants in Limerick City during this period were Hogan, Longbottom, Looney, Lynch & Spain, Neazor, O'Brien, O'Connor, O'Halloran, Prendergast, Rea, Sullivan and Thompson, though the below concentrates on the four major players.

The workers in these factories came together socially and formed the Victuallers Band. One of the requirements to enrol in this band was to be a pork butcher. This is now known as St John's Brass and Reed Band. They also formed other clubs such as factory rugby teams which competed against the other bacon factories in friendly matches.

THE MATTERSON FAMILY

J. Matterson & Sons bacon factory was established in 1816 by John Russell and Joseph Matterson, who were brother-in-laws of a kind, as both men married a Mossop sister, Mary and Eleanor. Mattersons operated out of Roches Street, while their rival company, O'Mara's, operated across the road on the same street from 1839 onwards. The two were separated only by Roches Row.

The company was run initially by Joseph Matterson Senior. On his death in 1854 Joseph Matterson Junior took over the Limerick aspect of the company while his other son, William Matterson, oversaw the London branch of the business. William Matterson died at the age of seventy-one, in London, in January 1903.

As well as his business interests, Joseph Matterson Junior was a key player in the Limerick community. He was vice-patron of the Protestant Young Men's Association, whose stained-glass window still remains in-situ on O'Connell Street.

Despite their wealth the Matterson family did not have luck in longevity. This is clearly evident in their obituaries from the *Limerick Chronicle* which are transcribed below:

12 Aug 1848, At Castletroy, Alfred, second son of Joseph Matterson Esq.

25 June 1853, At Casletroy, on Wednesday, aged 16 years, Mary the beloved daughter of Joseph Matterson Esq. of this city.

8 July 1854, Yesterday morning, at his residence, Castletroy, of a fever to the profound grief of his wife and children, Joseph Matterson, Esq. Provision merchant, the most enterprising and successful of our commercial citizens especially in the manufacturing of Limerick Hams, whose name is celebrated all over the empire. His remains will be interred in Killmurry church tomorrow morning at 8 o'clock.

26 July 1854, Sunday last, at Castletroy after a lingering illness, aged 20 years, Anne, eldest daughter of the late Joseph Matterson, Esq. of this city, having survived her beloved father only a fortnight.

23 January 1858, On the 20th instant, at Castletroy, Henry Matterson, Esq, aged 32 years, eldest son of the late Joseph Matterson Esq.

24 February 1858, This morning, at Castletroy, Miss Elizabeth Matterson, eldest daughter of the late Joseph Matterson Esq. aged 23.

1 June 1886, On 30 May, at Castletroy House, Mary, relict of the late Joseph Matterson Esq. in her 83rd year. Funeral will leave for Kilmurry Church at 12 o'clock on Wednesday.

Family of Joseph Matterson Junior:

12 September 1876, Sept. 11th, at 81, George Street Limerick, Henry Sutherland, aged 13 months, second son of Joseph Matterson, Esq.

4 January 1890, 3rd, at 81 George Street, Evelyn Gordon, third daughter of J. Matterson, aged 4 months.

5 May 1896, at Leonards-on-Sea, Mary Gordon (Molly) aged 17, eldest and dearly loved daughter of Joseph and Agnes Matterson, Castletroy House, Limerick. The funeral of the late Miss Mary Gordon Matterson, whose death occurred on Tuesday last at St Leonard-on-Sea, took place this afternoon. The remains arrived in Limerick by 1.30 train from Dublin and were bore to a hearse in waiting by some of the clerical staff of Messers Mattersons & Sons, and thence conveyed to the family burial ground at Kilmurry, where the interment took place. The cortege was of extremely large proportions and embraced all classes of the citizens and many country resident. While the mournful procession was passing through the city, the Protestant Young Men's Association and Chamber of Commerce were closed, while the monster houses and the other principal establishments in the city were shuttered. General signs of mourning and sympathy for the deceased's parents in their severe sorrow were exhibited in a marked degree

on all sides. The brothers of the deceased young lady were not present being just now abroad.

3 April 1906, We announce with very sincere regret the death of one of our leading and highly esteemed citizens Mr Joseph Matterson J.P. Castletroy House, who passed away yesterday morning at the County Infirmary. Mr Matterson successfully underwent an operation some ten days ago, but some time later his strength began to fail. Towards the close of the past week his condition was regarded as extremely grave. He gradually sank and passed away peacefully at 6:45 on Monday morning.

15 September 1932, We regret to record the death of Mrs Matterson, widow of Mr Joseph Matterson, J.P., of Castletroy House, Limerick, and senior principal of Messrs J. Mattersons and Sons Ltd., bacon curers, which took place on Monday in a nursing home in London. Mrs Matterson, who had reached an advanced age, had been for many years resident out of Limerick, but will be remembered as a lady who in her day took a prominent part in social life in this city, and her charm of manner made her very popular. On the arrival of the remains by motor from Dublin the funeral took place at 3pm this afternoon to Kilmurry, members of the family and many persona friends being present.

In 1901 Joseph Matterson Junior, aged sixty at the time, was living with his forty-six-year-old wife, Agnes, his children Leopold (eighteen), Vera Sunderland (nine), Victor (seven), Eva (five) and seven various servants. Joseph and Agnes were married for thirty-three years and had twelve children in total, with nine still living in 1911. After Joseph's death in 1906, Agnes and the remaining family moved to the Ennis Road. According to the census records her children Ian Gordon and Vera Sunderland were still living with her in 1911.

Joseph's brother, William Matterson, tended the London offices from at least 1871 onwards. He was married to Susan Pyle and had one son, William, who died in 1868 aged seven and one daughter, Ethel, who married Donald McKay in 1894. William passed away in his home in Kensington, London on 9 January 1903 aged seventy-one. William was buried in Norwood Cemetery, Lambeth, London, on the 13 January 1903. In his will he left £48,885 9s 8d split between his widow Susan, his brother Joseph and son-in-law Donald McKay, a major in the Royal Field Artillery.

> It is now nearly three months since I received your kind letter. Annie is very much pleased with her Valentine, she also received one from her cousin Eleanor and I do not remember if she answered her letter or not. I would have written sooner but I have had no servant for nearly four months so I am kept busy.

These were the first lines of a letter written by Limerick woman Eleanor McGhie, on 21 May 1873, to her niece, Mary Mossop, Joseph Matterson's wife, in Philadelphia. The letter she wrote used both sides of one sheet of paper, having filled the second side she turned to the first page again, rotating it by ninety degree and writing over the initial writing. This method of writing was known as 'cross writing' and was common practice during the Victorian era when postage was still charged by the page and writing paper was expensive. Occasionally letters were even re-crossed, which entailed writing the third and fourth pages in the crossed style and then returning to pages one/three, turning it forty-five degrees and cross writing once more. In this fashion six pages could be written onto one sheet, although in many cases this would render the letter almost illegible. Eleanor McGhie's letter, which was a folded sheet, filled three pages in straight writing and one in crossed. The result created a still quite clear and concise correspondence.

Along with the trivial information on family members' wellbeing, this letter also gave an all-too-brief account of the life of a Limerick woman in the 1870s. Eleanor McGhie (*née* Mossop) was born on 23 October 1823 in Cumbria, England. Her two aunts, Mary and Eleanor Mossop, married Joseph Matterson and John Russell respectively. These men arrived in London in 1816 to establish the Matterson's bacon factory. Soon after, in the 1830s, the three surviving Mossop brothers, which included Eleanor's father John, joined their sisters in Limerick. Eleanor married James McGhie, who was a miller and whose family ran the Blackwater mills. The Blackwater mills offices were based at 56 William Street, the address from which Eleanor's letter was posted. She had one child, a daughter, Ann McGhie, who was born 19 May 1862 in Limerick. By 1877, James McGhie had passed away and Eleanor was living at 31 Henry Street. Being married to a miller, she was considered a station below her Matterson and Russell relatives and although she would have been privy to many of the social events in Limerick, she would not have received a personal invitation.

In her letter she refers to the recent visit of the Lord Lieutenant of Ireland, John Poyntz Spencer, the third Earl Spencer, to Limerick to open a new gravel dock. On arriving in Limerick at half-past one in the afternoon of Tuesday the 13 May 1873 the Lord Lieutenant took luncheon at the residence of James Spaight on Georges Street. At three o'clock he arrived at the dock which was officially opened with a speech by the Harbour Commissioner. The Lord Lieutenant rose to make his speech but was interrupted by the jeers of a large crowd which had gathered to demand the release of political prisoners, and the return of Jeremiah O'Donovan Rossa. O'Donovan Rossa was the founder of the Phoenix Society which would later be incorporated into the Irish Republican Brotherhood (IRB) and who was exiled from Ireland and travelled to New

York in 1871. This riot would go no further than a vocal display as the ceremony had also been attended by the 64th Artillery Battalion and a troop of Lancers. The remaining ceremony ran smoothly and without incident.

Following the ceremony the lord and his wife were lead to the Model School where they were welcomed into the boys' room with a rendition of 'God save the Queen'. They then proceeded to the girls' room where two copybooks, including that of Eleanor McGhie's eleven-year-old daughter Annie, were inspected and duly complimented upon, the countess stating that 'they were very nicely written'. Following other spectacles and displays, Annie McGhie and two of her class mates were once again called upon, this time to recite 'Lady Clare', a poem written by Alfred Lord Tennyson who was poet laureate at the time, making this piece quite contemporary.

On the Wednesday a ball was held in honour of the Lord Lieutenant at the Limerick Country Club. Eleanor and Annie McGhie, although not in attendance, enjoyed much of the mood and revelry as their relations, the Matterson Russell and Gubbins families, prepared for the evening. The ball would last until two the following morning, after which the Lord Lieutenant rose at nine that day and made the short journey to fish at Doonass before returning to Dublin, later that day, by train from Castleconnell station.

Eleanor concludes her letter with the following light-hearted family mentions and well wishes:

> Mrs Matterson, Emily and Joseph are in London. Annie had a letter from E- this afternoon with a P-handkerchief enclosed, a birthday present. Joseph is going to be married this summer to a Miss Sutherland from Canady, She is Mrs. W Matterson's niece and came to London on a visit to her aunt about two months since. I sent a Cork Herald last week with the opening of the dock in it, I hope you get it. I addressed

it to your father and a Chronicle the week before to your uncle William. I dare say I shall be able to give you more news about the wedding next time. Annie joins me in fond love to both families.

Matterson Tragedy

In 28 May 1904, in the sausage department of Matterson & Sons bacon factory, twenty-year-old William Young of Hunts Lane was employed as a sausage filler. On this day he noticed that one of the machines was not working, so decided to take it upon himself to remove the belt and attempt a repair. He had been witnessed removing the belt using a ladder three times prior to this. According to factory regulations, a foreman should have used a pole to carry out the job of removing the belt in the evenings, as it was a specialised job. However, William got a ladder and placed it against the machine in preparation to remove the belt. He began to climb the ladder but his smock caught in the belt and he was carried around the machine at a speed of 135 revolutions per minute. When Dr George Myles attended the scene, William Young was being removed from the machine and it was discovered that both his legs had been separated from his body just below the knee and that he had died more or less instantaneously from the shock of his injuries. It was decided at the inquest that no blame should be attached to the firm or management as William Young acted without authorisation.

The matter of providing for the widow of the deceased was left up to the generosity of the owner of the factory, Mr Joseph Matterson. Unfortunately William Young's mother, Bridget, was a widow at the time of William's death and had already lost three of her five children; by 1911 her last child would also pass away, leaving her alone on Hunts Lane.

Mattersons closed their doors in Limerick for the final time in March 1983.

THE SHAW FAMILY

Shaw & Sons bacon factory operated out of Mulgrave Street. It was founded in 1831 by William John Shaw, whose family originated in Co. Down, Ireland. In 1892 the Shaw's factory, which proved to be well ahead of its time, was using electric lights, lifts, a mini-railway and even telephonic communications. Shaws became Clover Meats which closed their doors for the final time in 1976. The Shaw name was used by the Kerry Group following the closure of Clover Meats.

Below are the transcribed funeral notices from the *Limerick Chronicle* for members of William John Shaw's Family:

14 April 1868, On the 13th inst., at Rose Cottage, deeply lamented by a large circle of friends, Martha, the beloved wife of Wm. John Shaw, Esq. of this city. Her remains will be removed for interment at 8 o'clock on Thursday morning. She was buried in St Munchin's Graveyard.

2 December 1869, This morning at his residence, Rose Cottage, William John Shaw, Esq. His remains will be removed for interment at St Munchin's, on Sunday morning, at 9 o'clock.

30 August 1879, On the 28th inst. at Castletroy, the residence of William G. Gubbins, Esq. after a short illness, Harriett E. Shaw, second daughter of the late William John Shaw, Esq. of Willow Bank.

18 October 1892, On the 16th instant, at 2 Collingham Gardens, South Kensington, London, James Thompson Saw, eldest son of the late William John Shaw, of this city, and senior partner in the firm W.J. Shaw and Sons, age 51.

18 June 1918, The interment took place on Thursday, in Lackhampton Churchyard, of Miss Anna Gertrude Thompson Shaw, of Hereward, Shardington road who resided in Cheltenham for the past seven or eight years, and who died on Monday 10th aged 74 years. She was the eldest daughter of the late W.J. Shaw of Willow Bank Limerick.

William John Shaw's second son, Alexander William Shaw (27 October 1847 – 29 November 1923), was born in county Limerick and grew up in Derravoher, North Circular Road. He grew up to be a bacon curer and local politician and the founder of both the Limerick and Lahinch golf clubs. The family firm was already thriving when he took it over, but under his astute management it grew to become one of the largest bacon curing businesses in Europe, and Shaw became one of the most prominent businessmen in the city. Alexander's second son, Gordon Thompson Shaw, was killed in action on 28 August 1918 while serving as a captain in the 1st Royal Munster Fusiliers.

Shaw Tragedy

John Hogan, a thirty-five-year-old married man with five children who lived at Pump Lane, had been working at W.J. Shaw & Son factory on Mulgrave Street for twenty years. At ten in the morning on 5 May 1904 he was oiling the coupling of some machinery in the black pudding department when one of the wheels caught his jacket and he was twisted round rapidly while his feet, at each rotation, struck an overhead beam. Immediate action was taken to stop the machine but before this could be achieved John's legs had been broken off completely. He died almost instantly after his release from the grip of the whirling wheels. His funeral took place the following day at St Michael's church and he was buried in Mount Saint Laurence cemetery. All the management and employees of W.J. Shaw & Son factory were present at the funeral.

THE O'MARA FAMILY

J. O'Mara & Sons was founded by James O'Mara, who was born in Toomevara, Co. Tipperary. James O'Mara originally began curing bacon in the basement of his house on Mungert Street. In 1839 he moved his business to a purpose-built factory on 30 Roches Street at the junction of Anne Street, which happened to be across from their rival, Matterson's bacon factory. He also moved his family during this time to Hartstonge Street and later to Thomas Street. James was a member of the corporation, representing the Dock Ward, he was nominated for the position of mayor but declined the offer. He was a member of the Limerick Board of Guardians, a magistrate for the city as well as a visiting justice for both the male and female prison. He was of the Roman Catholic faith, a member of the Confraternity and a staunch nationalist.

James O'Mara's son Stephen O'Mara, born in 1844, was also a nationalist and supporter of the Home Rule movement. He served a term in prison in Limerick Gaol for refusing to give witness at Ballneety Crimes Court. He was elected a Member of Parliament and was Mayor of Limerick in 1885 and 1886. In Stephen O'Mara's will in 1926 he stipulated to his children that the shares of O'Mara's Ltd allotted to them were not to be sold except to other family members.

James O'Mara's son Joseph would become a popular opera singer. In 1904, he was touring with the Moody Manners Opera Company, performing the part of Jose in *Carmen* at the Kennington Theatre that season. In 1908, the Freedom of Limerick was conferred on Joseph O'Mara by Mayor Donnellan in recognition of his outstanding position in the musical world.

O'Mara's 100-year lease on the site on Roches Street ended on 18 June 1979 and the factory was demolished in the late 1980s to make way for the multi-storey which stands in the spot today.

Below are funeral notices from the *Limerick Chronicle* for members of James O'Mara's Family:

8 July 1893, The remains of the late Mr James O'Mara, son of Mr James O'Mara J.P, who died on Thursday at Peckham, London, after a short illness, arrived here today by the midday train from Dublin. At the station a very large number of citizens was assembled, including the Mayor and several members of the Corporation. The funeral took place at St Michael's Church with burial afterwards at Mount Saint Lawrence Cemetery.

20 April 1899, We announce this evening with deep regret the death of an old and most popular citizen, Mr James O'Mara. J.P., who passed away this afternoon at his residence, Thomas Street, in the 82nd year of his age. Mr O'Mara has been in failing health for a considerable time past, and, therefore his demise cannot said to be unexpected, but nevertheless the sad news has come upon all sections of the community with extreme sorrow. Mr, O'Mara was the head of the extensive bacon-curing establishment of J. O'Mara and Sons.

28 January 1905, After an illness extending a considerable period the death took place this morning at 11 o'clock of Miss Nannie O'Mara, Alexander Terrace. The deceased lady was the youngest child of the late Mr James O'Mara J.P., and throughout life had maintained a gentle and unassuming manner. She was ever the friend of the poor and needy, and in the circle of friends which she moved was regarded with the utmost affection. Among her own family her kindly counsel will be missed, and in the hour of their bereavement the sympathy of the citizens will go out to Ald. O'Mara and family in the loss they have sustained. The funeral will take place at 10 o'clock on Monday morning from Alexander Terrace.

27 July 1926, The death which we record with feeling of deep regret took place suddenly yesterday of Senator Stephen O'Mara. The deceased gentlemen had been in his offices, as was customary with him, in the morning, and not feeling well he proceeded to walk leisurely to his residence, Stand House. He was crossing Sarsfield Bridge at about half-past twelve, when he collapsed on the sidewalk. Pedestrians passing at the time rushed to his assistance and he was attended by Dr M. Graham who happened to be in the vicinity. Mr O'Mara was then semi-unconscious and was conveyed to residence in a motor car, where he passed away a short time later, after receiving the ministrations of his Church.

9 August 1927, The funeral of Mr Joseph O'Mara, the distinguished Irish tenor, took place yesterday morning after Requiem Mass in the Church of the Assumption, Booterstown, to Glasnevin Cemetery.

THE DENNY FAMILY

Denny's & Sons had one bacon factory operating out of 27 Upper William Street in 1891 and another operating out of Mulgrave Street. It was founded by Henry Denny in the 1870s and first operated as a Provision Merchants in Newtown Mahon, Upper William Street. Denny's & Sons later had premises in Limerick, Cork and Waterford. Denny's sausages makes an appearance in James Joyce's book *Ulysses*, where Leopold Bloom watches a young girl in Dlugacz's butcher's shop buy a pound and a half of Denny's sausages, as he waits to buy a pork kidney for his and wife Molly's breakfast. Denny's is now owned by the Kerry Food group, after they acquired it in 1982.

Below are the transcribed funeral notices from the *Limerick Chronicle*, for members of the Denny Family:

8 March 1892, Mr Abraham Denny, senior partner in the extensive bacon concerns at Limerick, Waterford and Cork died at his residence in Cahir, County Tipperary on Saturday. The deceased was Chairman of the Waterford Steamship Company and of the Waterford, Dungarvan, and Lismore, and Waterford and Tramore Railways.

21 January 1905, We regret to learn that on Saturday last the death took place, after a short illness, of Mr E.M. Denny, of Chiddingstone Castle, Kent (head of the well-known firm of Messrs. H. Denny & Sons, of London, Waterford, Cork and Limerick). Mr Denny, who had reached a ripe old age, was stopping at Bexhill in Sussex where his demise occurred. His funeral took place on Tuesday and the entire works at all the places above mentioned were closed as a mark of respect to his memory.

1 September 1927, The death is announced at his residence, Ballybardo, Cahir, of Mr C.E. Denny, head of the great bacon curing firm of that name, carrying on an extensive business in Waterford and Limerick and throughout Ireland and Great Britain. He had reached his 79th year, and was in enjoyment of good health up to a year ago. He is a great loss to the firm over whose destinies he had so long presided. Keenly interested in sport, he was an old supporter and ardent follower of the Tipperary Hunt, a patron of the Clonmel Horse Show and Clonmel Golf Club. A benign, kindly gentleman, he was a great favourite in South Tipperary, and his death is mourned by all who knew him.

Denny Tragedy

Three men were in the seed loft at Denny's bacon factory at half past five in the evening of 6 March 1895. The men were getting ready to leave for home when two of them,

Leabharlanna Poibli Chathair Bhaile Átha Cliath
Dublin City Public Libraries

John Lynch and Frank Delaney, started to play 'clowns', or in other words, started to mess around. During their antics, Lynch stood on a barrel and attempted to climb on Delaney's shoulders. The weight of John Lynch was too much for Delaney to support so he staggered and this caused John to overbalance and fall.

John Lynch hit the ground with his head and reportedly called out, 'Oh Frank, I am done!' These would prove to be his last words as he passed away soon after. Frank Delaney was arrested for his part in contributing to the death of John Lynch, but after evidence was heard at the inquest the charges were dropped. The funeral costs for the nineteen-year-old from Ellen Street were paid by the Denny company. John Lynch was buried in Mount Saint Lawrence Cemetery on 10 March 1895.

5

CRIME AND PUNISHMENT

LIMERICK NIGHT WATCHMEN

The night watchmen patrolled the streets of Limerick reporting on crimes and on problems which may cause crimes – such as doors and windows being ajar – and on things such as poor lighting, which could cause accidents. They would start at 9 p.m. and work until 7 a.m. the following morning.

They wore a uniform which consisted of a dark jacket with large buttons and a large buckled belt over dark trousers which were tucked into large boots. The regular watchmen also wore a 'custodian helmet' and carried a staff, while the inspectors wore a flat hat and had several bows on their jacket.

Though the watchmen were in charge of keeping the peace, sometimes they would find themselves on the wrong side of the law. In December of 1837 John Enright, a watchman on Mary Street, was accused of the murder of James Byrnes. At his trial it was decided that, as the principal witness was dead, the surgeon should give evidence first. The surgeon stated that the deceased had a wound to the left breast which would indicate a puncher wound by a penknife. As Enright was supposed to only have a watchman's pole in his possession the case was dismissed on this evidence and he was found not guilty.

The typical night's watch was a long, lonely, boring and tedious job, as can be seen in the recorded reports on one Sunday night in Limerick, 6 February 1848, where the following issues were reported by the watchmen on duty. The acting inspector that evening was Edward Browne, from whose handwritten reports detailed the following.

There was a total of twenty-two watchmen on duty that night, including: Mr Gallagher, who patrolled the Bank Place area, Mr Coffey, who patrolled the Nelson Street area, Mr Hayes, who patrolled the Carr Street area, Mr Mullins, who patrolled the Rutland Street area, Mr Sandes and Mr Fahy, who patrolled the Bedford Row area, Mr Stapleton, who patrolled the Thomas Street area and finally Mr Halpin, who patrolled the William Street area.

The men clocked in at 8.45 p.m. and set off on their respective beats. It was two hours before the first report came, when Fahy and Sandes brought John Smyth back to the station, charged by Gallaher with being drunk in the street. This was quickly followed by Halpin, reporting missing a piece of timber from Mr Boyd's new shop in William Street and Dr Cleary's back door not secured in Honan's Lane. An additional report came in stating that Mr McNamara's gate was left open in Upper Denmark Street.

At 10 p.m. Fahy was on his second arrest, this time one Edmund Gleeson, who was charged by Mrs McKnight with stealing a loaf of bread from her shop in Roches Street.

At 10.30 p.m. Hayes brought a padlock found loose on Mr Westropp's coach house gate in Griffin's Row. Meehan reported some twigging torn away from the gas lamp at Mr Carroll's house on Lower Cecil Street, and a bad light in said lamp. Coffey submitted reports of glass broken in the lamp at Nuiters and another pane broken in lamp at Myles, both in Nelson Street.

At 11 p.m. Enright reports on one Fanny Bromwell, who was charged by James Egan with a crime unknown.

At 12.30 a.m. Morgan reports that Mr Lautern's hallway door was found open in Thomas Street and Mr O'Neill's hallway door was open on Catherine Street. Meehan reports Mr Ryan's store door was not properly secured in Howley's Quay and Hayes reports that a fellow night watchmen, Hehir, found an abandoned handcart in the street and brought it to the station.

A 1.30 a.m. Hayes found a drunken seaman wandering aimlessly and brought him back to the station for his own protection, giving him a bed to sleep it off. Cusack reports that Mr Mackey's shop door was not secure in Cornwallis Street. Morgarin reports Mr Tinsley's hall door was not secure in the same street, Mr Lees shop shutters were not secured in High Street and James Lees window shutters were not secured in Play House Lane. Stapleton reports a missing knocker on Mr MacNamara's front door in Howley's Lane off Charlottes Quay. Stapleton also reports a bad light in the lamp at Tinsley's Store in Watergate Lane, a bad light in the lamp at the Slip on Bank Place and a bad light in the lamp in Charlotte's Quay. Additionally, he reported that at the corner of Bank Place Mr Purcell's front door was left open in Roches Street. Mongavin reports that Mr James Lee's front door was left open in Pike Lane.

At 2.30 a.m. Marshal reports Mr Gielding's front door was left open in Newenham Street.

At 3 a.m. Stapleton reports that the ricket of Mr Worrall's yard gate was open in Watergate Lane. O'Brien reports a bad light in the lamp at corner of a house near the post office in Rutland Street. Meehan reports a bad light in the following lamps: at the Cobbers Bulk, Bridge Commissioners Office, Spaights Store and all of the lamps on Henry Street. Fahy reports a bad light in the lamp in Old Watch house lane and a bad light in the lamp at O'Millies in Shannon Street. Meehan reports a bad light in the lamp at Miss E.B. Fitzgerald's in Lower Cecil Street and Mageniers reports a bad light in the lamp at Cuddy's in High Street.

At 5 a.m. Keating reports that Mr Anderson's front door was found open on Upper Mallow Street.

At 6.15 a.m. Hayes reports that a pane of glass was discovered broken in Mr Kearses Shop window in Upper Cecil Street.

The last report came in at 6.30 a.m., when Keogh reports hearing a great loud noise in Mr Donnoll's area in Quinlan's Street. While there was no other report as to what caused this great noise it would be interesting to speculate.

THE STATE OF THE CITY GAOL IN 1807

In 1807 the Crown carried out a general report on the state of the prisons in Ireland. The inspectors for the Limerick County and City Gaol were Messrs Sheppard and Gabbett and the head gaolers at the time were John Hedderman and William Spearing. The following report was submitted:

One building contains the prisoners for the County and City of Limerick. I had recommended to the Local Inspectors the necessity for an insulating wall, to protect the court walls of this Prison, in the angles of which sentinels should be placed. Had this advice been taken, the frequent escapes made since could not have happened. The Lodge, intended by the Architect for a Turnkey, is occupied by a military guard; the sentinel sometimes demands money for admitting persons to see their friends: I once experienced this impropriety, and complained to the Commanding Officer; it was then prohibited, but I am told it has been sometimes since practised. The Gaol is kept clean. The imprisoned Debtors in this County and City did not get the County allowance of bread as Felons do. At my visit in October last, I remonstrated with the Inspectors on the severity of this distinction, and prevailed on the County Inspector to distribute to six very poor Debtors, whose friends lived at a considerable distance from town. This kind practice he has continued. The Inspector over the City Prisoners, gave sensible reasons for not complying with my desire, but said a charitable society, established in Limerick, took the poor Debtors into their care, compounded their debts, and relieved them by weekly donations of money.

141 Prisoners were tried at both Assizes; 18 were convicted, 5 capitally, 4 of whom were executed. 43 Crown Prisoners and 16 Debtors were in custody on 1st January 1808 and 55 cases were dismissed.

1850 CASES

As far as criminal cases are concerned, 1850 was an especially tough year in Limerick. In the week ending 21 September alone there were 4,595 people in the city workhouses, which was a decrease on the 6,850 in February when Harvey's warehouse on Upper William Street was converted to a temporary workhouse.

There were several reports of rioting in the streets. The bread cart of Bannatyne (of Limerick) and Ryan (of Bruree) were attacked and plundered by a crowd of men and women in Irish Town in February, which led to bread carts being escorted by the police through this area of the city.

In February all the shops in both St Mary's and St John's parish were shut for a few weeks due to their windows being broken and goods stolen.

Crimes and punishment were rife, and some of the punishments seem, by today's standard, both harsh and bizarre, as the following accounts will show.

Fifteen-year-old John Fitzpatrick and his accomplice, sixteen-year-old John Hickey, were caught stealing waistcoats, the property of one Mister John Bassett on 22 August 1850. Both boys were found guilty and sentenced to one month in Jail at hard labour and to be whipped three times.

While it seems a harsh sentence, these boys could count themselves lucky as on the same day two women, Anne Torpy, thirty, described as being 5 feet 1 inch tall, with brown hair, and Johanne Kelly twenty-five, 5 feet 1½ inches tall with black hair, were found guilty of stealing the wearing apparel of P. O'Connor, and were sentenced to seven years' transportation. Anne Torpy had earlier that year been convicted and imprisoned for six months for larceny along with her younger brother, Thomas Torpy. Both Anne and Johanne were sent to Grangegorman Female Prison in Dublin where they were removed from Ireland on the *Black Friars* ship.

Anne Stundon, at the age of fifteen, found herself in court for a second time for theft in March 1846. She had previously spent four months in jail, but this time her punishment for stealing a pair of boots would be much more severe. For this crime the 4 feet 10 inch tall blonde-haired, blue-eyed girl would first be sent to Grangegorman Female Prison where she was the youngest woman in the prison. From here she was transported from these shores for seven years to Australia.

The following was recorded in the *Limerick Chronicle* on Saturday 29 June 1850:

1850 County Quarter Sessions – Thursday
The Assistant Barrister, having concluded the civil business of the Court at one o'clock, directed the prisoners in custody to be arraigned, when the following pleaded guilty, and were sentenced:

John Twomey, stealing silver spoons, the property of Thomas Browning, Esq., of Crass, seven years transportation.
John Barron, stealing wearing apparel at Ballinacurra, to be transported for seven years.
Eliza O'Brien, larceny of clothes at Thomastown, being an old offender, was sentenced to seven years transportation.
Bridget Bourke, stealing wearing apparel from Bridget Morony, two months imprisonment.
Joseph Freeman, stealing shoes, one month.
Daniel O'Connell, stealing hay, the property of Bryan O'Donnell, of Ballinagaddy, one month.
Patrick Reilly, stealing feathers, the property of Michael McMahon, of Scart, one month.

Mary Carroll, stealing a coat from John Frawley, of Bruff, one week.

Patrick Halihan, stealing shirts, the property of Joesph Slattery, to be imprisoned three months at hard labour.

Thomas Condon, stealing a shirt from Mathew McNamara, one month at do.

John Magee, stealing two iron wheel barrows, the property of M. Gilbertson, Kilmallock, three months.

Margaret Leary, stealing vegetables, the property of Laurence Bourke, of Drombana, one week.

Julia Welsh, larceny of kitchen utensils, one month.

Margaret Collins, larceny of a gown, one month.

Edmond Condon and John Dwyer, stealing a cow, the property William Gubbins, 15 years transportation.

Patrick Purcell, stealing wearing apparel from Mary Hogan, 3 months at hard labour.

Anthony Regan, Denis Coffee, Michael Sullivan, stealing grass, one week each and to be whipped.

John Hayfield, stealing flannel, the property of Jas. Ryan, 6 months imprisonment, and three times whipped.

Margaret Sheehan and Anne Childerhouse, stealing milk, the property of M. Hayes, of Mungret, one week's imprisonment.

Maurice O'Gorman, stealing iron, the property of Michael Gubbins, at Ballinacurra, one fortnight.

John Lenane, stealing shirts, a fortnight imprisonment and to be well whipped.

M. Connor, larceny of iron, a fortnight imprisonment and to be well whipped.

Michael Shea, larceny, one week at hard labour.

Bryan Corkery, stealing an iron gate from Timothy Ryan, of Pallasgrean, six months imprisonment at hard labour and to be well whipped.

John Tuomey, stealing a lamb, six months hard labour.

John and Connor Ryan, larceny of wearing apparel from Patk. McCormack, on 8 May, one week.

Michael Riordan, stealing an iron gate from Revd Joseph Gabbett, of Fairfield, one week.

John Scully, stealing a shirt from John Devitt of Abington, a fortnight.

Bridget Carroll, stealing a cow from John Ryan of Abington, one week.

Catherine Bourke, stealing fowl, one week.

James Moran, stealing wearing apparel, the property of the Killmallock guardians, do.

Hanora Carthy, larceny of a sheet, one month at hard labour.

David Nagle, stealing iron, the property of the Kilmallock guardians, one fortnight's imprisonment, and to be whipped.

1850 City Quarter Sessions – Friday

At 10 o'clock the day before, the mayor took his seat on the Bench with the Assistant Barrister, when the City Grand Jury were sworn for Crown business: Richard. B. Corneille, foreman; Robert Unthank, Leslie Acheson, John C Drysdale, John Fogerty, Edward Goodwin, John James, Richard Miller, Eugene O'Callaghan, John F. O'Gorman, Martin O'Donnell, Robert O'Shaughnessy, Samuel Alexander and James Alexander, Esqrs.

His Worship in addressing them said, 'Gentlemen of the City Grand Jury, the calendar is of such a nature as to require no observation from me. I perceive however, that serious riots have occurred in the central and auxiliary workhouse. Bills of indictment will go before you against some of the parties implicated in these disgraceful disturbances, and I have to request you will give them your best attention, as the offence is one of a very serious and aggravated nature; and should the prisoners be found guilty by the verdict of a Jury, they will be severely punished. It is a great aggravation of their crime, to find that persons who have been maintained at the expense of the industrious rate-payers of the union should be so unmindful of their position and devoid of gratitude as to cause such annoyance in the City, and I trust you will fully investigate the charges preferred against them. There is nothing else that needs comment as I am sure every case will receive your best consideration. The bills will be sent up now.'

After the City Grand Jury had retired to their room, it was announced that the County Criminal business would be resumed, a Jury being empanelled, the following convictions took place, after which the court adjourned at six o'clock that evening:

William Hickey, found guilty of stealing two sheep, the property of William Fitzgerald, of Grange, was sentenced to 7 years transportation.

Thomas Gleeson, an ungrateful servant in the employment of Francis Greene, Esq., of Greenmount, who was a kind benefactor to the offender, was sentenced to 12 months imprisonment, at hard labour, and to be twice well whipped, for larceny of oats.

Johanna Slattery, stealing pawn tickets from Margaret Guinnane, to be imprisoned two months at hard labour.

William Duggan, convicted of stealing money and keys from William Dinneen, of Ballylanders, was sentenced to 7 years transportation.

W. Hickey, stealing a lamb from Sarah Nash, being an old offender, was sentenced to 7 years transportation.

Cornelius Bresnehan, larceny of £3 from Timothy Connolly, to be transported 7 years.

Cornelius Moore, stealing a cow from Daniel Collins, of Drombana, 7 years transportation.

Hannah Hartigan and Mary Murphy, apprehended by Mr Sheils, Inspector of the town watch, were sentenced to 15 years transportation for stealing a cow the property of Michael Lynch, of Drombana. Also, Mary,

Ellen and Michael Quin, same rule, for stealing a cow
the property of Michael Lynch. One of the prisoners
prayed 'bad luck' to his worship.

Thomas Connors, larceny of shirts from Margaret
Shine, one month imprisonment.

October 1850
The following are convictions reported in the
Limerick Chronicle on the 30 October 1850:

Edmond Hannan, a notorious pickpocket, was convicted
of stealing a purse of money from Mrs Pierce Creagh in
George's Street on 13 July, and sentenced to seven years'
transportation. However, the transportation records show that
the convict was ordered to be discharged 15 January 1855.

Michael Mannix, employed in the bakery concerns of
James D. Lyons, Esq., was indicted for embezzling money to
the amount of £15, which he had received from customers in
the name of Mr Lyons. The evidence against the prisoner was
his own admission to the clerk, who arrested him at Killonan
station, from whence he was about to leave for America.
He was sentenced to be imprisoned for nine months with hard
labour.

Patrick O'Dea, a servant, was found guilty of stealing
a pair of boots from his former master, Dr Gore,
and sentenced to one month's imprisonment.

Patrick Davern, a young man in the employ of Messrs.
Evans and Curtis, George's Street, was indicted for an
assault on Patrick Keane, who was also a salesman in the
same establishment. The case was proved by Patrick Keane,
who sustained severe injury in the face, having been struck
with a ewer by the traverser, in his bedroom. Mr John
Horgan and Dr O'Shaughnessy were the other witnesses
examined. The jury found a verdict of common assault and
the court ruled a fine of £5 or one month's imprisonment.
The fine was paid.

At the prosecution of Mr Hugh Wrightson, verger, William Merritt and Thomas Sheehy were convicted of stealing lead off the porch of St Mary's Cathedral and sentenced to six months' imprisonment at hard labour and to be whipped three times.

James Higgins and James Tuohy, were found guilty of stealing lead off the roof of Mr D. O'Connor's house, North Strand, and sentenced to seven years' transportation each. According to the Transportation records, James Higgins died in Phillipstown Gaol, King's County on 24 August 1853 while James Tuohy was discharged on 9 February 1855.

Patrick Doyle was convicted of stealing lead off a house on Sir Harry's Mall, the property of Francis Dwyer, and sentenced to seven years' transportation. He was discharged on 12 May 1855.

Patrick Gilligan, John Hayes and John Glinn were found guilty upon same indictment but, it being their first offence, were only sentenced to six months' imprisonment each with hard labour and to be whipped three times.

John Burns was found guilty of stealing lead off a house in High Street and sentenced to like punishment.

William Gleeson was convicted of stealing lead of an unoccupied house on Cecil Street and sentenced to seven years' transportation.

Mary Kelly, a Cyprian, was found guilty of stealing a bank post bill for £5 from William Barnard of the Foot Artillery. She was imprisoned for six months with hard labour.

Patrick Sullivan and Ellen McCarthy pleaded guilty of stealing several shirts, bacon, and wearing apparel from the residence of Revd John Brahan, parish priest of St Mary's church. They were each sentenced to seven years' transportation. According to the Transportation records, Patrick Sullivan died in Spike Island Gaol, County Cork 27 June 1854.

Winifred Foley was found guilty of having three waistcoats, which were stolen from the residence of

Mr J. Bassett, Rutland Street and sentenced to two months' imprisonment with hard labour. John Fitzpatrick and John Hickey by whom the articles were stolen were sentenced to one month's imprisonment and to be whipped three times.

Mary Savage was found guilty of stealing a cloak, the property of Mary Forest and imprisoned for one month.

Mary Purcell was found guilty of cutting the pocket off Mary Purcell (repeated name in source) at the Dominican Chapel on Sunday 18 August, during the celebration of Mass. The Assistant Barrister said the offence was committed under circumstances at which, it should be supposed, a Christian would shrink with horror. The sentence was that she be transported for seven years.

Mary Connell was found guilty of stealing a purse of money and some manuscript papers from Mr James B. Fortune, commercial traveller and imprisoned for one month with hard labour.

James Griffin and Denis Hayes were convicted of stealing 30 stone of potatoes, the property of Mr Denis McNamara at Corbally and sentenced to six months' imprisonment with hard labour and to be whipped three times.

Margaret Roohan was convicted of a riot and stone throwing at William Street auxiliary workhouse, where she was an inmate, but discharged as she had been in custody since June.

Transportation punished both major and petty crimes in Great Britain and Ireland from the seventeenth century until well into the nineteenth century. The penal system required the convicts to work on government projects such as road construction, building works and mining, or they were assigned to free individuals as unpaid labour. Women were expected to work as domestic servants and farm labourers. While transportation from Britain/Ireland officially ended in 1868, transportations to Australia had ceased fifteen years previous to this.

In a case heard in Limerick in February 1867, Peter H. Maguire, who was a private in the 74th Regiment, was charged with the larceny of a flannel shirt from the shop of Anne Ryan in Patrick Street. Anne told the court that Peter H. Maguire walked into her shop, took the shirt and walked towards the door. She asked him for the shirt and he refused, telling her to send for the police or a watchman. He told her that he wanted to get out of the regiment and that he took the shirt in order to be incarcerated or transported. He was imprisoned for one month and was told he would have to return to the regiment once his time was served.

All women who were sentenced to transportation in Ireland in the mid-nineteenth century were sent to the prison in Grangegorman Female Penitentiary in Stoneybatter Dublin, where they had to spend three months learning skills that would make them employable once they were transported.

At the same time as harsh sentences, such as transportation for petty theft, were being meted out there were also what seemed to be incredibly light sentences for heinous crimes. The murder of Alice McCormack at Lock Quay, by her husband Michael in 1846 resulted in him serving just one year in jail.

Not all trials were so heinous, as in the case of Mary Anne Williams versus Mary Anne Tracey over a pair of mittens, a case that was actually thrown out of court.

HANGINGS

The Good Shepherd Laundry, located on Pennywell Road in Limerick, is built on the former Farrancroghy execution site, where public hangings took place in the eighteenth century. The hangings were later conducted at the gaol, or prison, when it was officially opened in 1832. In the period between 1835 and 1899 there were 237 people executed in Ireland; twenty-five of those were executed in Limerick.

In April 1835 four hangings took place within the gaol walls. First there was thirty-five-year-old Michael Quinlan, convicted of the rape of Mary Connars, then Daniel Malony, Matthew Malony and Jeremiah O'Donnell for the attempted murder of Thadeus Ryan. Two years later, in 1837, Mary Cooney found the hangman's noose for the murder of one Anne Anderson. Mary was the disgruntled former employee of the victim. After losing her job for stealing blankets, she had fallen on hard times and ended up resorting to prostitution. Anne was the elderly widow of Captain John Anderson, 4th Garrison Battalion. She was living alone on Harstonge Street at the time of her murder. Mary Cooney, who was in her late forties, was described as being 'quite meanly dressed, and of aspect and manners very repulsive'.

In 1847 there was a fatal case of mistaken identity that rocked Limerick's justice system. Michael Howard was arrested and charged with the murder of Johanna Hourigan and her son, Conor Hourigan. When found guilty and sentenced to death by the hangman's noose, Michael adamantly proclaimed his innocence whenever given the chance to have his voice heard.

Michael is on record stating, 'I do solemnly declare in the presence of Almighty God, in whose presence I will shortly appear, that I had no knowledge, act, or part in the murder for which I am about to suffer. And further, I do solemnly declare that I had no knowledge of, nor did I give my consent to write a memorial in which it was set forth that I acknowledged my guilt.' This well-phrased and heart-felt declaration ultimately fell on deaf ears and the young man was hung by the neck until dead on 1 September 1847 while a very large crowd of 6,000 watched.

It would later be discovered, unfortunately too late, that he was innocent. As coincidence would have it, there was another Michael Howard in Limerick, who was of no relation what-so-ever to the first, and it was he who murdered the

mother and child. This Michael Howard was apprehended and, after being questioned by guards, pleaded guilty to the crime. The real murderer was due to be hanged for his crime on 22 February 1848, but was reprieved and sent to Smithfield, from where, in exchange for his life, he was transported, for the rest of his natural life, to America.

February 1848 was yet another busy time for the hangman in Limerick, this time with five men convicted of murder, William Ryan (Puck), Andrew Dea, John Renihan, James Skeahon and James Quaine. The latter two were convicted of the murder of Ralph Hill, a reposition agent.

First there was Andrew Dea, 'a handsome lad, of mild innocent aspect'. He was a mere nineteen years old when he walked to the scaffold, holding a Bible in his hand from which he read litanies and prayers. He was convicted of shooting dead his former landlord after his family were evicted from their farm. Later that day, twenty-three-year-old Ryan was also executed. He had only learned to read while in gaol for another offence the year before, when he shot a man's horse while taking part in a robbery.

Professor Barnett and Mr Falkener, from England, took casts of Ryan and Dea's heads to present at Phrenological Societies. It was noted in the press at the time that there were 'not two heads (within the range of rational persons) which present more different developments than the heads of these two criminals'.

In another case, John Renihan, who reportedly appeared 'stupidly indifferent and regardless of the awful judgement impending over him' was hanged for the murder of J. McInerney. It was reported that while waiting for the execution a number of men and boys amused themselves by killing rats.

At exactly 2 p.m. on 20 April 1848 two men were lead to the gallows of the county gaol. First to be hanged was Thomas Fitzgerald, convicted for the shooting and savage beating of John McEniry, who he left for dead (though the man survived until the following day). Fitzgerald pleaded innocent to any knowledge of this murder. Second, Michael Ryan, whose hanging was a painful experience, for the accidental murder of Hanora Ryan who was shot while saving her husband from the gunman's bullet.

On 11 August 1849 there were three executions, including a woman, Catherine Dillion, and her lover, John Fogerty, who was married with six children, who were hanged for the savage beating of Catherine's husband who was stoned and beaten with a hatchet. John Fogerty's elderly mother was in the audience but did not shed a tear when he dropped. Catherine Dillion, unlike most who were hanged on the gaol grounds, was not buried within its walls but was taken by her family to be waked by hundreds. John Freven, 'a tall handsome young man', was also hanged that day, for the murder of Peter Nash.

The following year two young brothers, William (seventeen), and Matthew Gavin (nineteen), were executed for the murder of John Ryan. The execution of the Gavin Brothers in 1850 was watched by the Gavins' surviving brother and a few thousand people, mostly women. Mingling with the crowd were pick-pockets who were reportedly very active.

On 23 September 1851 Michael Hanly (thirty-four), was hanged for the murder of his wife Ellen Hanly. His co-accused was Mary Fahy, but her hanging was suspended due to her being pregnant. It was estimated that at least 20,000 people turned out to see the fall of this man. Ellen Hanly was beaten with a hatchet and had a rock tied about her before she was thrown into the canal by Troy's Lock. Michael was estranged from his wife and had been living with Mary Fahy, aged twenty-three, for some time. The couple were preparing to sail to America when they were arrested.

There was not another hanging in the city for seven years, when, at 7 a.m. on 20 October 1858, John Cullinan was hanged for the murder of Elizabeth Giles. His wife was in the small crowd which had gathered, holding his child in her arms and lamenting loudly throughout. He had murdered Elizabeth Giles, who was on her way to visit her daughter who would shortly be leaving for Australia, in order to rob her of what he thought was a larger sum that she had on her.

In 1862 three men were found guilty of the murder of Francis Fitzgerald, a landowner, in a dispute about rents. These men were sixty-one-year-old Thomas Beckham, twenty-one-year-old James Walsh, and Denis Dillane, who was executed the following year. Beckham and Walsh had initially invaded capture and had been on the run with £300 bounty on their heads, but were soon arrested. Thomas Beckham was very excitable on the morning of his execution, rushing after the nuns who had attended him calling, 'All is right now'. Following this he gave two young boys who were attending the priests a threepence piece each, telling them 'take that in remembrance of me'. As he stood on the gallows he exclaimed that he was 'no spy or turncoat' to which his son in the crowd cried out, 'Bravo Father, I knew you would die true!' and the crowd cheered. It was only the Tuesday before his death that he married the woman with whom he lived for twenty-five years.

For the execution of Walsh the crowd was about 3,000 strong. Walsh had woken the morning of his execution a little perplexed at 6 a.m., saying 'sure they didn't hang Beckham until 12 o'clock in the day'.

Later it was discovered that Denis Dillane, who was fifty-five years old, had hired Beckham and Walsh to murder Fitzgerald and so he too met his end by the hangman's rope.

The final two men hanged in the nineteenth century in Limerick were Thomas Cuncean (thirty-five) in 1879 for the murder of Johanna Hay and Francis Hynes (twenty-three) in 1882 for the murder of John Dougherty.

In the 1920s there were three men who were executed by firing squad in Limerick. These were Thomas Keane in 6 June 1921 and Cornelius McMahon and Patrick Hennessey on 20 January 1923. All were convicted for being members of the IRA volunteers. The latter two men were originally from Ennis, County Clare.

Although there was other Limerick murderers executed these took place in Mountjoy, Dublin and not in Limerick. These included people such as Annie Walsh (thirty) and her nephew Michael Talbot (twenty-four) who were hanged on 5 August 1925 for the murder of her husband Ned Walsh (sixty-one).

The last person executed in Ireland was Limerick man Michael Manning (twenty-five) on the 20 April 1954, for the rape and murder of Catherine Cooper, aged sixty.

6

GRAVEYARDS

You can tell a lot about a person by the markers which are left on their departure from this world. The final marker for many is their grave.

ST MICHAEL'S,
HIDDEN IN THE CITY

Across from the city library, which is housed in a building known as The Granary, and behind a wall, lies one of the oldest, most unknown graveyards in the city. The church which stood here was probably a Norman foundation and was in ruins by the early seventeenth century. It was totally dismantled prior to the Cromwellian siege of 1651.

Once the entrance way is located, and one finds themselves in the midst of the graveyard, it's hard not to feel like you've been transplanted out of the heart of the city into a secret garden that possesses the final resting place of hundreds of souls. The graveyard was used until the late nineteenth century, and while most of the grave stones located here are so old that their words are no longer legible after centuries of weather, some can still be read.

This beautifully concealed place holds such testimonials as:

This stone was erected by Michael Ryan in memory of his son James Ryan who Dept. this life 4th of January 1781 aged 9 years.

And:

Pray for the soul of Catherine Barry of Dunvion who departed this life Feb 12, 1766 aged 92 years.

ST JOHN'S AND THE TOMB USED FOR AN OFFICE

The existing St John's, Church of Ireland, was built in 1851, though a church has existed on this site since the twelfth century. The graveyard surrounding the church was built just off Johns Square and includes a large limestone mausoleum, built in 1873. This tomb was to be the final resting place of the Norris family, and, unlike most, was the house of the living before becoming the home of the dead. John Norris Russell, a merchant who also became a ship-owner and industrialist, used his tomb as a city office. He built the Newtown Pery Mills on Russell's Quay and the Newtown Pery store adjacent to it on Henry Street. He was also one of the founders of the Savings Bank.

The mausoleum, located to the north of the church grounds, flush with the boundary enclosing the site, was an abutting two-storey structure. It possessed a square-headed door opening with limestone architrave. It had a panelled cast-iron door leaf with vent holes to upper panels and a cast-iron relief goat figure above a ribbon band with raised lettering, reading 'Che Sara Sara 1873'. Another limestone plaque to the side reads:

Here Lieth the Mortal Remains of Francis Russell Who Died the 25th day of August 1800. He was an

Affectionate Husband a Kind and Indulgent Parent a true friend & an honest Man.

Yet another plaque reads:

John Norris Russell Dedicated this Monument to his Father Francis Russell A tender Husband An affectionate Parent A kind Friend & an honest Man.

ST MUNCHIN AND THE SHIPS

On 12 April 1868, Gulbran Olsen Berge departed Christiania in Oslo, Norway for Quebec aboard the Norwegian emigrant sailing ship, *Hannah Parr*. Berge left behind a wife, Karen (Bue) Berge, and several children in Gudbrandsdalen Valley, Norway, and made his way to the United States to secure a new life for his family. The ship's list, published on the Norway Heritage website, recorded his passenger information as: Gulbrand Olsen Berget, thirty-two, married – Residence Gausdal, Gudbrandsdalen.

The voyage of the *Hannah Parr* should have been just another routine crossing, despite primitive conditions that were common aboard early emigrant ships, but it ended up being one of the better documented sailing voyages in the history of early Norwegian-American migrations because of its exceptional nature.

Shortly after leaving Norway, the *Hannah Parr* encountered severe weather when it reached the mid-Atlantic. On the second day of the storm, a large wave over the stern took out the pilothouse and its gear, as well as the kitchen, and left the ship with hardly any riggings or sail.

Gulbran Berge kept a diary throughout the voyage, though it consisted of mostly short reports about weather conditions. His descriptions became more extensive during and after the storm. For 27–28 April 1868, his notes read:

> We ran into a bad storm that lasted 2 days, and everyone thought they would die. The storm began the night of the 28th and lasted until 12 o'clock midnight of the 29th. We lost almost everything that was on the deck. The captain's quarters were completely wrecked. The kitchen was washed overboard. The sails and riggings were destroyed by the wind.

The captain would have been blown off the ship if the one who steered the boat had not rescued him. The foremast was blown off, but we made some use of it. The captain said he had never been in such a storm before. He had never heard of another emigrant ship that it had happened to like it did to us. Three people were hurt, and some were so tired because they had not slept for 72 hours.

Unable to continue on its journey, the ship limped slowly back to Ireland, where it docked for repairs at Limerick in May.

About 400 passengers were aboard the ship, and these people found themselves having to depend on the citizens of Limerick for hospitality while repairs were carried out.

According to *the Limerick Chronicle* of 9 May 1868:

No accident occurred to crew or passengers, all on board are in excellent health, and as fine a looking lot as one could see. Every provision was made for their comfort by the Norwegian consul, Mr. M. R. Ryan, who has visited them, and seen after their wants. The vessel is placed in consignment of Messrs Ryan, Brothers, & Co., who are getting repairs completed energetically.

In a letter to the editor, a worried citizen, Mr James Walsh, expressed this concern for the emigrants with the following:

It has been ascertained that a considerable number of the Norwegian emigrants at present among us furnish an occasion for the exercise of the Christian liberality of the people of Limerick. There are, in fact, about 40 or 50 of very slender means among them.

By 21 May repairs were still dragging on and the Norwegians were becoming depressed, but luckily, Limerick had the answer:

Inmates of the female Blind Asylum attended as a choir to lead in the singing of the hymns, and they were accompanied on a beautiful harmonium by one of the number, who is proficient in music. The harmonium was kindly and gratuitously lent for the occasion by Mr. P. Corbett, of George-street, who with characteristic generosity, declined payment from the committee.

While the *Hannah Parr* was undergoing repairs, there was a great deal of interaction between the traumatized Norwegian emigrants and their curious, hospitable, and lively Irish hosts. Berge wrote:

7 May, Many came on board to sell food and other things. They took up the anchor, and since no steamboat had come we continued on our way because we had the tide with us … In between the rivers it was very pretty. The leaves, potatoes, and corn were as big as they were in mid-summer in Norway. When we came ashore we were met by many people, and they looked at us like we had come from another world. They followed us around so much we could hardly move. At night three or four men had to keep watch on deck, and every day hundreds of people came to look at the ship without sails.

May 10, [We] all wished to go on a trip on the railroad for a few miles inland, and this was an enjoyable trip. Some gentlemen treated us to 40 pints of Port wine which was all drunk up, and some felt happy from it [most likely a translation mistake, since letters by other passengers mention 'porter' (beer)].

May 11, When we were in Limerick we had a very good time. The people did all they could to make it pleasant for us … Two hundred of us went to the theatre, and even though none of us understood what they said, we enjoyed it.

The work on the ship went slow … we were laid up there about six weeks. We sailed from Limerick the 9th of June, and although we were not ready we had to leave because the tide would go out so no ship could come in or go out for 10 days. We transferred to a steamship four miles out of town where we cast anchor to get ourselves entirely ready, and we thought we would be there only a few days. While we were anchored there, most of the passengers had to send word back to Limerick for food because we left in such a hurry we didn't get time to buy all we needed.

After departing the Irish coast to face the Atlantic once again, the Norwegian emigrants found that new passengers accompanied them on the remainder of the voyage, namely lice and the dreaded disease, typhoid fever. However, only a few deaths resulted.

A plaque hangs in St Munchin's in honour of the children from Norwegian ship wreck, which reads:

The Norwegian emigrant ship 'Hannah Parr' desmasted & severely storm damaged was towed into Limerick docks in May 1868. This plaque is dedicated to the memory of the three Norwegian children who died shortly after arrival and are interred in this churchyard, also to the kindness and generosity of Mrs. Ann Kearse and many other Limerick people who cared for the 400 passengers and crew. This plaque was erected by the Limerick Civic Trust and unveil by H.E. Mr. Truls Hanevold, Ambassador of Norway to Ireland on 22nd September 2008.

KILQUANE AND THE TRAITOR

The tale of the McAdam family, who were buried in Kilquane, Corbally, began during the 1690 siege of Limerick, when the Williamites were nearing the Shannon in Corbally. Philip McAdam, who was supposedly employed as a fisherman, plotted to destroy the Irish defences by leading the enemy to the only safe place to cross the Shannon. McAdam 'feigned sickness' and remained behind at the banks of the Shannon as the other fishermen, on 'fearing the cruelty of Williams soldiers', had fled to Clare or to the woods in Cratloe. The Williamite army, seeking the advantage of a suitable fording point at which to cross the Shannon, one of the cities natural defences, approached McAdam with an offer. One account states that he was 'handsomely rewarded for his treachery' against the Irish by receiving 'a large tract of land in the vicinity' from the Williamites. While an alternative version of the tale sees McAdam in a more favourable light, in which he was forced to either show the Williamites the crossing point on the Shannon and receive 'a keg of gold' or refuse and face 'a block and headsman's axe'.

The fishermen with whom he was associated never forgot this treachery and would visit the family grave in Kilquane, desecrating it while repeating the following poems:

> Here lies the body of McAdam the Traitor,
> Who lived a fisherman, and died a deceiver,
> The devil came for him in flashes of thunder,
> And now he is in hell and it is no wonder.
> Here lies the grave of McAdam the traitor,
> Who's burning in hell with the thirst,
> And anyone who don't desecrate his grave,
> I pray that their belly burst.

> McAdams nose is long
> McAdams nose is strong
> It would be no disgrace
> To McAdams face
> If McAdams nose was gone.

ST BRIDGET'S ON THE HILL

In 1842, when the new workhouse on the Shelbourne road was completed, the guardians would never have imagined the great influx that would be upon them with the arrival of the potato blight in Ireland and the onset of the Great Famine, which lasted from 1845 to 1850.

For the first few years after the opening of the workhouse the poorest of the poor were buried in the old Killeely graveyard, but this soon became overcrowded, and as dogs invaded the graveyard for night raids on bones, it was decided that a new graveyard was needed. So the plot of land behind Watchhouse Cross was leased in 1849 and burials began.

The area was a boggy marsh, and to accommodate the burials a huge pit 12 feet deep was dug. Into this pit the bodies went in sixes, each layer separated by a thin covering of soil and some lime. This lime would react with the bodies, increasing the rate of decomposition. Over 5,000 unnamed souls are buried here, their only marking a single wooden cross.

KILLEELY OLD GRAVEYARD

Killeely Graveyard is now surrounded by houses on all sides, though this ancient graveyard had been in use for many centuries prior to the urbanisation of the area. In this graveyard is buried John Meany (1902–1982), a man who it was believed fathered eighty-nine children. His family plot dates from at least 1720. Also interred here in 1807 was the renowned surgeon Sylvester O'Halloran, who specialised in eye surgery and developed a new method of treating cataracts (see p.40).

ST MARY'S AND THE PRINCE

In the front of St Mary's Cathedral graveyard there is a small, unassuming headstone facing the river erected in honour of His Royal Highness, Prince Milo of Montenegro of the Royal House of Petrovic-Njgos.

Prince Milo was born in 3 October 1887 and died on 22 November 1978. He studied at the Military Academy in St Petersburg, Russia. He was a personal friend of Tsar Nicholas II and Tsarina Alexandra and was present when his cousin, Princess Stana, introduced the infamous Rasputin to the imperial family. He was deposed in 1919 and fled from his homeland to the USA. He married Helena Smith in Santa Barbara, California on 3 September 1927. On 23 October 1928, his only child, a daughter, Milena was born in Los Angeles.

Late in his life he settled in the West of Ireland. In his last Will and Testament he asked to be buried in the grounds of St Mary's Cathedral, Limerick and his dying wish was carried out.

PUMP LANE AND
THE SOCIETY OF FRIENDS

The Limerick Society of Friends (the Quakers) kept meticulous burial records for the Pump Lane Graveyard, which was once situated at the end of Pump Lane in English Town. Pump Lane is now known as St Francis Place and the graveyard is located under St Mary's Girls Primary School.

Not all those who were buried here were in fact members of the Quaker community, which speaks to the good and accepting nature of the Quakers. Some had asked permission, or their families had asked permission for them to be buried in the graveyard, while others were previously disowned members who were granted special permission to be interred there.

Jane Mark, aged thirty-six, the wife of John Mark of George Street, died on the 13 April 1812 and was the first recorded burial in Pump Lane on the 2 May 1812.

That same day Richard Desmanoiss, the ten-month-old son of French teacher James Desmanoiss, passed away. James asked permission for his son to be buried in Pump Lane on the 3 May 1812, even though he was not a member of the Quaker society.

The third and final burial of 1812 took place on the 21 October when eighty-four-year-old Sarah Toomey of Francis Street, who had died two days before, was interred.

In 1813 and 1814 three burials took place in Pump Lane. None of these were members of the Quaker society although George Alleyn, a fifty-six-year-old master cooper from Old Clare Street, who was buried on the 25 November 1814, was once a member but he had been disowned by the Quakers.

William Sheppard, a sixty-year-old from St Michael's parish, was one of the last to be buried in Pump Lane on the 19 June 1833.

He was followed by another William on the 18 August 1833, William McAllister, aged eighty-nine from Glentworth Street.

The last burial recorded in Pump Lane was that of John Hill, aged fifty-seven, from St Michael's parish, on the 22 October 1833.

The Society of Friends graveyard is now situated on the Ballinacurra Road, on a section land known as the 'Quaker Field' and was moved to this location in the 1870s. This land was donated by Joseph Massey Harvey, whose wife Rebecca was the first to be interred there, on 8 July 1833. She had passed away on Christmas Day 1831 and was temporarily buried in the grounds of her house in Summerville until the new burial ground was prepared. Later Joseph Harvey and several of his children were also interred here.

UNDERFOOT AT SIR HARRY'S MALL

On Sir Harry's Mall by Baals Bridge, the majority of Gaelchoaliste students go about their studies unaware of what lies beneath their feet. For centuries this site was outside the city walls and when plague hit the dead would be buried here. There were almost a 100 bodies in this site before the walls fell and development started. Their graves were soon forgotten as people continued with their lives above ground. It was only in the 2000s, when construction began on the Gaelcholiaste building, that these graves were discovered, almost 100 men, women and children.

MOUNT SAINT LAWRENCE AND THE WOMEN OF THE FIRST WORLD WAR

On 4 August 1914 Britain declared war on Germany and with this the armies of men left their home to fight, leaving behind their women and children. By 1917 the amount of men remaining available to serve was drastically reduced, and so women were recruited for service and the Women's Army Auxiliary Corps (WAAC) was formed. This marked the first time in British history that women were employed by the army in a non-nursing capacity. On 31 March 1917 the first women in the WAAC were sent to the battlefields in France, totalling fourteen cooks and waitresses. The WAAC later became the Queen Mary's Army Auxiliary Corps (QMAAC) when Queen Mary became its patron. It was in this regiment that many Limerick women would serve, showing a lot of courage, grit and determination. Below is the history of three Limerick women who died while serving in the QMAAC during the First World War.

Mary Agnes McMahon, known as Agnes, was born in 1896 and was the middle child of Michael and Mary McMahon's five children. In 1911 Agnes was working in

Cleeves Condensed Milk Factory, while her father and brothers were railway servants. The family moved around Limerick in 1901: they were living in Lady's Lane, in 1911 in Lee's Lane and by 1918 in 14 Prospect, Rosbrien. Agnes would have seen her brothers heading off to war and on seeing the posters calling women too Agnes packed up her bags and headed to the Officer's Cadet School in Kildare. She served with QMAAC under the service number 18691. She was ranked as a volunteer when she died, aged twenty-two, on the 27 October 1918 at 14 Ellen Street Limerick. She was buried in Mount St Lawrence Cemetery on 29 October 1918.

Mary Eva Wallace, born in 1899, was the daughter of W. Wallace, who, in 1919, lived at 4 Roches Street, Limerick. Mary was a volunteer member of the QMAAC, and her service number was 17526. On 14 March 1919, at twenty years of age, she died in Dublin. Her remains were removed to Mount St Lawrence Cemetery for burial on 16 March 1919. She is also mentioned on the Grangegorman Memorial in Dublin.

Mary E. Daly, aged thirty-five, a volunteer member of the QMAAC, died 5 June 1919 in the National Hospital, Hammersmith, London. She was buried in Mount St Lawrence Cemetery on 7 June 1919.

7

LIMERICK AND THE QUAKERS

The sixteenth and seventeenth centuries were a tumultuous time of political and religious upheaval throughout Europe. Many people had become disillusioned with the mainstream Christian churches, namely the Anglicans, Roman Catholics and the Puritan and new denominations were popping up all over the place, some of them, such as Baptists and Quakers, stood the test of time while others vanished as quickly as they appeared.

The Quakers, or as they are formally known, The Religious Society of Friends, were founded in England in 1652 by George Fox. George Fox, who was a shoemaker by trade, travelled the length of England by horseback, preaching to those he met. The principle on which the Quaker faith was founded was the idea that every individual could experience God without external guidance from any other person. They endeavoured to live simple, industrious, sober and honest lives while advocating freedom of religious choice and equality of the sexes. On the whole, Quakers were an educated group who prided themselves on keeping meticulous records. They kept records on nearly everything, from births to deaths, major events, scandals, or anything else they deemed important that was going on around them. There were no paid ministers and they managed the church themselves through a community effort, while 'Elders' are appointed to look after the spiritual wellbeing of the other Quakers.

THE QUAKERS IN LIMERICK

It was not long before this group began to travel and are on record as preaching for the first time in Ireland in 1654, in Lurgan, Co. Armagh. A year later they held their first meeting in Limerick, in the house of Richard Pearce, a local apothecary. Within a year the Quaker population in Limerick rose to seventy people. Throughout these early years the home of Thomas Holmes was used for worship. Worship would take place in complete silence, allowing each individual to find and commune with God on their own terms. Both Thomas Holmes and Richard Pearce's houses were in Bow Lane in the Englishtown. Other prominent Quaker family names in Limerick were Harvey, Fisher, Tavernor, Unthank, Alexander, Bennis and Hill but many of these names no longer exist in Limerick today.

QUAKER PERSECUTION

It was not long before the Quakers began to attract the attention of the local churches and persecution of the Quakers was rampant in the seventeenth century, to such an extent that the governor of Limerick, Henry Ingoldsby, in 1656, banned the public from interacting with members of the Quakers under penalty of banishment from the city. Despite the governor's threat, during their first fifty years in Limerick the Quakers were forced to pay tithes to the established Church of Ireland parishes to which they belonged.

The Quakers kept a record of some of the persecutions they faced throughout this time in what they called the *Book of Sufferings*. In 1656, for example, Quaker member Edward Tavernor was fined £2 because he would not serve on a jury, as not swearing an oath is one of the rules of the Quaker faith. Later in 1660, eight Quakers were committed to Limerick Gaol for three weeks because they practised their religion. Furthermore, in 1662 Limerick local Edward Kemp was forced out of the city after refusing to pay £10 for the upkeep of a church. His house was seized by the bishop and his wife and children were subsequently evicted.

Despite the brutal treatment they faced, in 1671, a community in Limerick had grown sufficiently for a meeting house to be erected in Creagh Lane, after King Charles II granted the Quakers limited religious liberties. The Quakers continued to utilise the meeting house on Creagh Lane for over 130 years.

In 1682 in Pennsylvania, a group of Quaker men from Limerick, among them Samuel Tavenor, James Craven, Richard Pierce and Thomas Phelps, were granted 1,000 acres each by William Penn, the founder of the state. These men had suffered persecution in Limerick. For example, Thomas Phelps' shop had been continually burgled and on one occasion a rope had been put about his neck and he was almost hanged to death.

By 1687, three members of the Limerick Corporation were Quakers; they were Samuel Tavernor, James Craven and William Craven.

During the 1690–1 Siege of Limerick, the Quakers brought alms to Jacobite and Williamite alike and after the Treaty of Limerick was signed the Quakers were treated with far greater tolerance within the city.

QUAKER TRADITIONS

The Quakers maintained a tight-knit community and a network of committees which operated both nationally and internationally. This was an advantage to the Limerick Quakers, who operated as merchants and could thus effectively purchase and transport goods from Limerick to much further afield. If Quakers wished to marry the couple would have to obtain 'clearances' from the other members of the society. To do this they would have to declare their intent to marry in front of both the men's and women's meetings. Marrying outside of the society was cause for expulsion.

In December 1816 James Fisher and Mary Harvey became engaged in accordance with the rules of the Quakers; they attended both the Men's Monthly Meeting and the Women's Monthly Meeting to declare their intent. Both their parents were required to give consent to the marriage at these meetings, where it would be decided if the union would be allowed. Following this, the marriage took place on 16 January 1817. Mary Hill attended the wedding and reported back to the Women's Monthly Meeting in February that 'good order was preserved there and at the house the same day and evening'.

Siblings were often of different religions during the early period of conversion. This is best illustrated with the tale of Thomas Story and his brother George Story, who were both born in Cumberland, England. Thomas would later move to America and George to Limerick. In 1716, Thomas Story and William Penn, notable Quaker leaders, travelled from America to Limerick to spread news of the society and to attend Limerick Quaker meetings to glean information on the local community. Another reason Thomas Story chose Limerick as a visiting stop on their tour was to visit his brother, who had been appointed the Dean of Limerick's Anglican Church in 1705. A huge crowd of people turned out to see the brothers, since at the time it was deemed quite extraordinary for siblings to be so acclaimed in different religions.

The Quaker community was known for taking care of each other. This can be seen in cases such as Thomas Jellico in 1771, who was unable to work due to illness and whose plight was recorded in the *Book of Suffering*. A fellow Quaker, John Taverner, offered to give him 2s 8½d during his confinement, but it was decided by the rest of the community that this donation should be reduced to one shilling and seven and a half pence to encourage Thomas Jellico to recover quickly and to return to work.

Just as Quakers will take care of their own, they will also attempt to protect their community as a whole, even if it means disowning members. In 1787 it was decided that Joshua Sheppard, quoted as having 'misconduct as of so heinous and reproachful a nature', was to be publicly disowned as to distance the Quakers from the scandal he caused. He was accused by the society for staying out late at night and keeping unreasonable company which ultimately lead to an incident where he was in a fight with his neighbour, who was subsequently maimed. Joshua Sheppard left the city quickly and in disgrace.

When a member of the Quakers moved it was recorded in the *Notices of Removals* book in the monthly meetings. It contained details of where members had moved from and to, as well as a reference letter from their previous community. As in this message from Youghal about Anne Sheppard, who was moving to Limerick in October 1796: 'we believe her to be a young woman of pretty orderly conduct ... she left us clear of debt and marriage engagement, as a member in unity we recommend her to your friendly care.'

In 1805 the Quakers moved their meeting house to Cecil Street, and paid an annual rent of £28 44s.

CHARITY WORK

Not only did the Quakers strive to attend the needs of members of their own community, they also did their best to extend a hand to members of the greater society in which they dwelled. During the famine periods the Quakers ethos would come to the fore, with assistance to the poor and less fortunate distributed across the country. They were some of the first to react to the seriousness of the Great

Famine in 1846 by setting up Soup Kitchens in Limerick as well as in Waterford, Enniscorthy, Clonmel and Youghal.

Although they wished to aid the needs of the poor to a greater extent, the Quaker community in Ireland at the time was only about 3,000 people strong, while the population of Ireland in the 1840s was over 8 million. However, through their community networks they managed to raise the equivalent of £14 million from Quakers living abroad in relief funds for those in need.

The Quaker group responsible for the care of the poor during the famine were called The Limerick Auxiliary Committee and they were responsible for eleven soup boilers in County Limerick and six in County Clare. They also distributed almost 1,200 tons of food to the community. Unlike other religious societies, who administered to the famine victims in an effort to win them over as new converts, the Quakers did not force the destitute to convert in order to obtain food.

In June 1847, the Quakers reportedly gave the parish of St Patrick's at Corbally two bags of rice, two bags of biscuits, two bags of peas and two whitewash brushes; additionally it gave the parish of St Patrick's at Garryowen four bags of meal, two bags of rice, two bags of peas and two brushes.

Despite the massive effort of the Quakers during this time, it is reported by the Royal Irish Constabulary that approximately 400,000 people died in the winter of 1846–7 due to the lack of food. One can only imagine how much higher that number would have been had it not been for the helping hand of the Quaker society.

Many Quakers suffered ill-health themselves while aiding the hungry during the Great Famine. For example James Harvey who died in 1848 aged forty-eight years, James Philips Evans aged forty-seven years, William Woods aged forty-seven, and others, like Deborah Unthank who died the same year, aged ninety-two years and Deborah Alexander, aged eighty-six years.

HARVEY'S QUAY

Another great contribution of the Quakers can be seen on the very streets of Limerick today due to their industriousness and keen eye for business. Many of the Quaker families in Limerick were merchants and helped to build areas of the city. The street, now known as Harvey's Quay, began as two separate Quay's named after the men who constructed the areas in the 1820s. The original Harvey's Quay was located between Bedford Row and Lower Cecil Street. This quay was named after Reuben Harvey, who constructed that portion on a section of land leased to his father, Joseph Massey Harvey (1764–1834), by Lord Viscount Pery in 1791.

The additional section, from Bedford Row to Sarsfield Bridge, was then known as Fisher's Quay, and was originally constructed by James Fisher on land leased in 1791. The lease of Fisher's Quay was subsequently transferred to William Gabbett in 1857. On the lease for the quays there was the following stipulation: 'The Grantee convenants to keep in repair the premises, the accidents of fire, war and general rebellion only excepted.'

From the time the areas were built until the early twentieth century the quays were primarily used for the loading and unloading of goods with the majority of buildings being storehouses. The two quays were eventually merged and by the mid-twentieth century it was known only as Harvey's Quay. The above named streets are presently merging again and the entire quay section is now often referred to as Howley's Quay. The following list is from the trade directories for Harvey's Quay from 1838 to 1886 of other businesses operating in the street:

1838 – Mr Crilley, baker; John Crilley, spirit merchant; William Crilley, ship chandlers; and J. Ryan, tailor and habit maker.

1846–86 – Robert Talbot and his son William Talbot, block and pump makers. (In 1859 Robert Talbot took a young lad Thomas Case of John Square to court for leaving his apprenticeship early. Thomas subsequently served one month in jail with hard labour before returning to his apprenticeship. Robert Talbot was taken to court himself seven years later for unpaid rates.) In 1886 William Talbot also operated here as a bicycle and tricycle agent.

1846–56 – Eliza Ryan, public house.

1856 – William Ryan, tailor.

1870 – Timothy Morrissey, spirit merchant. (In 1868 Timothy was fined for having his public house open out of hours.)

1875 – M. Dawson and Son, iron merchant; John McDonnell, unknown.

1886 – James Belle, refreshment rooms.

Both men, Reuben Harvey and James Fisher, were Quakers as well as being members of the Chambers of Commerce. Reuben Harvey (1789–1866) was the eldest son of Joseph Massey Harvey and Rebecca Mark. They had relocated from Cork to Summerville House, just off the South Circular Road in Limerick and it was here that their eleven children were. Summerville House is now part of the Mary Immaculate College, which was founded in 1898.

Joseph was an entrepreneur and had petitioned for a new bridge crossing the Shannon in 1822 while he was the head of the Limerick Chamber of Commerce. This bridge was completed in 1835 and is now known as Sarsfield Bridge. He was a well-respected citizen throughout his life and later passed away at his daughter Hannah Todhunter's home in Dublin. He was returned to Limerick for burial in the graveyard he had donated to the Quakers following the death of his wife Rebecca in 1831. She had been the first interred in the new graveyard, on 8 July 1833.

Reuben married Hannah Christy and they had three children: James (1820–1837) who died as the result of a fever aged only seventeen, Mary Christy (1825–1858) and Joseph (1826–1887). As well as his business on Harvey's Quay, Reuben also operated the Plassey Mill for a period while living at Plassey House, Castletroy before selling it to Richard Russell. He died on 21 September 1866 in Pery Square at the age of seventy-seven.

Two of Joseph Massey Harvey's other sons, Joseph Harvey (1793–1836) and the Irish botanist William Henry Harvey (1811–1866), both served as the Colonial Treasurer in Cape Town. Joseph had initially been appointed as Colonial Treasurer by Thomas Spring Rice in 1835 but this post did not suit him and he decided to return home with his family. Sadly he passed away on the way back to Limerick from Cape Town onboard the ship, *Triumph*. William Henry was appointed to the position following the death of his brother and he would spend the next seven years in Cape Town.

In his successful career William Henry Harvey described over 750 newly discovered species of plants and in excess of seventy-five genera of algae. Between 1833 and 1862 he wrote over thirty papers on the subject of botany. Although he criticised Charles Darwin's theory of evolution, Darwin still praised him as a great botanist. As an adult he was disowned from the Quakers Society for joining the Anglican Church. In 1861 he married his childhood friend Elizabeth Lecky Phelps, though this marriage was short lived as he passed away five years later of tuberculosis in Torquay, Devon.

Another of Joseph Massey Harvey's sons, Jacob Harvey (1797–1848), moved to America in 1816. He married the daughter of David Hosack, a well-known New York doctor who attended Alexander Hamilton, one of the Founding Fathers of the United States after his ill-fated duel with Aaron Burr.

8

WHO'S WHO

Limerick has created some very well-known personalities in many various fields, including opera singers such as Catherine Hayes and Joseph O'Mara, actors like Richard Harris, and personalities such as Terry Wogan. The following are a few other Limerick personalities that left an impression in their respective fields.

ANDREW CHERRY

Andrew Cherry was born the eldest son of John Cherry, a printer and bookseller, on 11 January 1762. He was born on the site of the former post office on Bridge Street and was raised a member of the Society of Friends. He received a good education in Limerick and, at the age of eleven, was apprenticed to James Potts, a printer, in Dame Street, Dublin.

From a young age Andrew acquired a taste for the stage. This was partially due to James Potts love of the arts, who would seldom attend the theatre without young Andrew with him. At fourteen Andrew Cherry made his first appearance as Lucia in the tragedy *Cato* in a large room at the Blackmoor's Head Tower Street, Dublin. At seventeen he abandoned his apprenticeship to take up theatre life full time. He played his first independent performance in Naas, in a company of strolling players (which consisted primarily of runaways), only to return to Dublin after a short interval, half-starved and penniless. This did not deter him and, after a few years' steady theatre work, he joined the Company of Theatrical, which was managed by Richard William Knipe, who had abandoned a life in law for the stage. After Knipe's sudden death in 24 March 1779, Andrew Cherry married his daughter in 1783. He travelled successfully with a company

of actors through Ireland for about six years where he was known as Little Cherry.

Andrew Cherry's opera, *The Outcast* (1796), was produced in Drury Lane, London. At Belfast he acquired considerable reputation, and in 1797 he won success at the Theatre Royal, Dublin. He then accepted engagements in England, and his performance at Bath was pronounced 'as finished a picture of the scenic art as had ever been performed on their boards.' In 1802 he appeared at Drury Lane, London and in 1804 produced *The Soldier's Daughter*. Other pieces followed, and he continued to act at Drury Lane until it was burned down in 1809.

After this Andrew took a company to Wales, with Edmund Kean as leading actor. On 7 February 1812 in Monmouth, Wales, Andrew Cherry passed away aged fifty. His legacy lives on in Limerick where a street was named after him Cherry Place, on Kings Island. Cherry Place is also known as Crosbie Row.

His best-known song was 'The Dear Little Shamrock of Ireland', which was brought into the twentieth century by Irish tenor John McCormack. Some of his other works include: *Harlequin on the Stocks*, 1793; *Poor Bess and Little Dick*, 1796; *Life Epitomised and the Soldier's Daughter*, 1804, *All for Fame or a Peep at the Times and Spanish Dollars*, 1805; *The Travellers or Music's Fascination* and 'Thalia's Tears' (a sketch) 1806; *Peter the Great* and *A Day in London*, 1807.

ADA REHAN

World-famous Shakespearean actress, Ada C. Rehan was born Delia Crehan on 22 April 1857 (though on many records she was shown as being born in 1860) in Shannon Street, Limerick. Her parents were Thomas Crehan (born in 1820), a ship carpenter and Harriet Crehan (born in 1822). The family were Protestant and relocated to Brooklyn, New York with Delia in 1864. Delia was a statuesque 5 foot 8 inches, with grey blue eyes and dark brown hair. William Winter, dramatic critic and author, wrote:

> Her physical beauty was of the kind that appears in portraits of women by Romney and Gainsborough – ample, opulent, and bewitching – and it was enriched by the enchantment of superb animal spirits.

By 1870 her elder brother William (born in 1845) had followed in his father's footsteps and was working as a ship carpenter, while her elder sisters Mary (born in 1848) and Harriet (born in 1850) were working as actresses. Delia and her younger brother Arthur (born in 1860) were scholars, but by 1880 they too would be recorded as actors. She also had another brother, John (born in 1854). It is unsurprising that Delia followed her sisters into acting as by 1870 Mary's husband, Oliver Byron, was also an actor and living in the Crehan household in Brooklyn in 1870.

It was her brother in law, Oliver Doud Byron, who helped her make her debut in 1873 as Clara in *Across the Continent*. Rehan then joined Mrs Drew's celebrated ensemble at the Arch Street Theatre. It was during this period that the typographical error dropped the first letter of her surname, Crehan, giving her the stage name that she would be known as Ada C. Rehan.

She spent two seasons with Drew before being spotted by John Augustin Daly, an American playwright and theatre manager. Daly was so impressed with her performance in 1879 as Mary Standish in his plays *Pique* and *L'Assommoir*, that he asked her to join his company in New York. Her first performance with Daly was as Nelly Beers in *Love's Young Dream* and under his guidance Rehan quickly became the finest and probably the most beloved of all younger comediennes.

She was living with her parents and brothers William and Arthur in New York in 1880. Their name was spelled Creghen, according to the records of the time.

Regan excelled at classic comedy, including such Shakespearean roles as Mrs Ford, Katherine, Helena, Rosalind, Viola, and Beatrice and Sheridan's Lady Teazle. But she was also at home in the newer comedies Daly presented, among them the American premiers of Pinero's *The Magistrate* (1885) and *Dandy Dick* (1887), in which she played Mrs Posket and Georgiana Tidman respectively.

William Winter was quoted as saying:

> Her acting, if closely scrutinized, was seen to have been studied; yet it always seemed spontaneous; her handsome, ingenuous, winning countenance informed it with sympathy, while her voice – copious, tender, and wonderfully musical – filled it with emotion, speaking always from the heart.

Miss Rehan was the model for a solid silver statue of Justice that was presented as part of the state of Montana's mining exhibition at the World's Columbian Exposition in Chicago in 1893.

After applying for a passport in 1894 for the purpose of 'travelling on the Continent', Ada Rehan was widely admired in Europe, having acted in Paris, Berlin, Hamburg, London, Edinburgh, Dublin, and Stratford-on-Avon.

Following the death of her mentor, manager and director John Augustin Daly, in 1899, Ada would slowly drift from public appearances until she officially left the stage in 1906 and made New York City her home until her death there in 1916. She is buried in Green-wood Cemetery, Brooklyn, New York. Her funeral arrangements were announced in the *New York Times*. Even though she had left Limerick's shore more than fifty years previously she was still remembered in an obituary from the *Limerick Chronicle*,

11 January 1916, where her birth name was given as Charlotte Rehan.

She was written about in the following: *Ada Rehan: A Study by William Winter* (a private print for A. Daly, 1898) and *Ten Weeks with Ada Rehan* by Lark Taylor (1916).

More than twenty-five years after she died, a Second World War liberty ship was named after her, the USS *Ada Rehan*.

LIAM REDMOND

Liam Redmond was born in Limerick on 27 July 1913, the youngest child of Thomas Redmond and Ellen McAlister. His father was a Sligo-born carpenter who also taught woodwork and technical graphics; his mother was born in Louth. The couple married in Armagh in 1902 and lived in Dublin for a period where they had their first child Mary. They then moved to Limerick in about 1905 where they would have their remaining four children, Ellen, John, Thomas and finally Liam. In 1911 the family were living in Ballinacurra.

Liam Redmond attended a Christian Brothers primary and secondary school in Dublin. After secondary school his sights were set on a medical degree from the University College, Dublin, though he later changed his major to drama. Noted playwright and poet William Butler Yeats attended one of Liam's productions at the college and, sensing Liam's talent, Yeats invited him to join the Abbey Theatre in 1935 as a guest producer. Yeats went on to write his play *Death of Cuchullain* specifically for Liam to produce.

In the same year, 1935, Liam made his Abbey Theatre acting debut in Sean O'Casey's *The Silver Tassie*. In 1939, he made his first stage appearance in New York in *The White Steed*. He left America at the outbreak of the Second World War and played regularly on the London stage, returning from time to time to the Abbey for a season or performance. Some of his more sterling performances over time included *The Playboy of the Western World*, *Juno and the Paycock*, *The Square Ring*, *The Doctor's Dilemma*, *Loot* and *The Island*.

The actor joined the Dublin Verse-Speaking Society and occasionally read poetry on radio. In the 1950s Liam went back to New York to play Canon McCooey in *The Wayward Saint* on Broadway, which won him the George Jean Nathan Award for his performance.

Liam was a well-rounded actor which led him easily into roles both on film and television. He was a regular on such British TV series such as *Z Cars*, *Douglas Fairbanks Jr, Presents*, *Swizzlewick*, *You're Only Young Twice* and *The Avengers*. His extensive filmography can be seen below. He was often a requested actor for the likes of Walt Disney and played opposite Elvis in *Kid Galahad*.

Liam Redford retired to a quiet life in Dublin in the late 1970s, following a decade of declining health, and later passed away aged seventy-six in Dublin on 28 October 1989. He was married to Barbara MacDonagh (17 August 1936– 17 November 1987), who he had met while he was the director of the Dramatic Society and she was the secretary.

CONSTANCE SMITH

A strikingly attractive, but troubled Irish actress, Constance Smith, was born in 46 Wolfe Tone Street, Limerick on 7 February 1929. The eldest of eleven children, her father Sylvester Smith, was a foot soldier in the Irish Army. Her father also worked on the Ardnacrusha Scheme during the 1920s and was a native of Dublin. Her mother Mary Biggane was a Limerick native. Constance's father died in 1944 when she was fifteen years old, and because her mother was unable to support her as well as her ten siblings (many of whom passed away at a young age), Constance was sent to a convent.

Her first break began with her winning a 1946 look-a-like competition in a Dublin movie magazine, touting her as a dead ringer for Hedy Lamarr. Afterwards, her mother sent her photograph to a film studio. She was called for a screen test, which she was reluctant to take but did so under her mother's insistence. The screen test was successful and she was contracted to the Rank Organisation. In the process of being groomed by the Rank 'charm school', Constance first demonstrated her fiery temperament and unwillingness to toe the line. This quickly got her fired.

In 1950, after playing an Irish maid in *The Mudlark*, she was spotted by 20th Century Fox which offered her a contract.

Upon her arrival in Hollywood, producer Darryl F. Zanuck cast her opposite Tyrone Power in *I'll Never Forget You* (1951). However, Power soon decided she was not experienced enough and replaced her with Ann Blyth. Constance was most active in the 1950s, appearing in Hollywood features such as *Man in the Attic* (1953) and also as a presenter for the Academy Awards ceremony in 1952.

On 1 February 1951, Constance married Bryan Forbes, an English film director, actor and writer, whom she had known for three years. They married in Caxton Hall, London, when Forbes was twenty-four years old. The newlyweds were never able to go on honeymoon as Forbes had to report immediately to his play, *The Holly and the Ivy*, and she to Tyrone Power for her film, *The House in the Square*.

Constance regularly clashed with producers and executives, starting with her refusal to change her surname from 'Smith' to something more memorable to movie-going audiences and, by the time her contract expired in 1953, the studio had forced her to undergo an abortion. After this she continually failed to get the parts she felt were worthy of her abilities and she began an embittered descent into a life of drugs and alcohol. In June 1955 Constance divorced Forbes upon charges of desertion. Forbes went on to marry fellow British actress, Nanette Newman, the same year.

Constance's last films, all minor, were made in Italy between 1955 and 1959 and included a role as Lucretia Borgia in *La congiura dei Borgia* (1959). During her time in Rome in 1958, she first attempted suicide by overdosing on barbiturates.

In 1960 she paid a visit to Limerick, with her producer and soon to be live-in boyfriend Paul Rotha, where she received a grand welcome which was widely publicised. Paul Rotha was a documentary maker and film historian and was over twenty years her senior. Two years later, in 1962, Constance was sentenced to three months in prison for stabbing him. On 4 February 1968, she stabbed Rotha for the second time and was charged with attempted murder. Oddly enough, Constance and Rotha later married in 1974. Paul Rotha died 7 March 1984, Wallingford, Oxfordshire.

Constance Smith's tumultuous life continued in a downward spiral. She tried several more times to kill herself and her last decades were spent in and out of hospitals. When able to get herself together for brief periods, she worked as a cleaner. Constance died 30 June 2003 of natural causes in obscurity, in Islington, London. Constance's remains were cremated and her ashes were scattered in Rose Garden of the crematorium in London. A sadder end is hard to imagine.

9

LOVE AND MARRIAGE

Limerick is said to be a lady. While that may be true, Limerick is a fickle lady when it comes to matters of the heart. According to the Bible, love is patient and kind; love is not arrogant or rude; love is not irritable or resentful and above all else, love never ends. Well, that may be true for the rest of the world, but Lady Limerick is jealous, she is foolish and above all else, she is vengeful in the case of love.

Below are just a few stories which illustrate the deep-seated and passionate love affairs that have gone horribly wrong throughout Limerick's colourful history.

ACCIDENTAL BIGOTRY

Although Daniel Robinson was an educated man, he was above all else a self-centred rogue. His tale begins in 1841, when he was twenty-six years old, on the fateful day he met Anne Griffith, a young Roman Catholic girl.

Now this is where Daniel's difficulties began as he was of the Church of Ireland faith and inter-religious love affairs were not common practice at this time. Regardless of societal pressures, Daniel and Anne moved in together, an act which inevitably led to Anne getting pregnant. Upon hearing about the situation, Anne's parish priest, Revd John

Madden, immediately married the couple in order to 'take them out of this course of sin'. In 1842 their son William was born. Domestic life with Anne did not suit Daniel, who very shortly after the birth of his son left his new family to lead the solitary life of a bachelor once more.

Cupid once again shot an arrow through Daniel's heart the following year when, on 16 September, he married Herminia McDonough (aka Southerwood) in St Michael's

Church of Ireland. Unfortunately for Daniel, he forgot to first seek a divorce from his first wife, Anne.

News soon broke of this second marriage and Revd John Madden reported young Daniel to the authorities as a bigamist. The extraordinary case was brought before the Limerick Assizes in 1844. As a sign of the time and the religious dogma that was institutionalised, it was decided by Mr Justice Jackson that, 'The sacred institution of marriage is considered by the law to be null, in the case of persons of different creeds being united by any minister but one of the establishment'. In this case, the established church was Church of Ireland and on the heels of this judgement, the jury found Daniel not guilty.

Daniel and Herminia went on to have at least two children: Daniel Southwell Robinson in 1852 and Edwin Robinson, who was baptised on 28 May 1860 in Church of Christ-Congregational, Limerick, a Presbyterian church.

LOVE AND LOSS

The course of true love did not run smoothly for Mary McDonnell, a young single Limerick woman in the early 1800s. Mary had her eyes set on a handsome tradesman named Patrick Grady, and she refused to let anyone or anything stand in the way of her dream romance with him. Even though Patrick continually refused her advances, it did not stop Mary from begging and pleading with him to become her spouse. She was so head-over-heels in love with him, she just could not take no for an answer.

On Monday night, 7 February 1831, Mary vainly urged Patrick again, only to be once more heartbreakingly rebuffed. This last rejection proved to be too much for her sensitive soul and moments later she ran from his arms and flung herself into the canal between the two bridges, Baals and Mathew, and drowned.

This was not the only case of a lover's tiff which caused heartache and tragic loss in the city. John Lyddy, a fisherman, and Sarah Russell Lyddy were happily married in 1892. They lived in a house on Flag Lane, which was located just off John Street in Limerick. On the last days of 1896 the city was rocked by the couple's double fatality which left their three small children, Mary, Christopher and John, orphaned.

At 12.40 a.m. on Thursday, 28 December 1896, when Sarah was twenty-two and John was twenty-six, night-watchman John Ryan was going about his duties in the Clare Street area when he heard a couple arguing outside Quilligan's public house on the corner of Broad Street and Lock Quay. He did not interfere but soon heard the woman shout at her husband to let her free. However, when he did she ran to the Lock Quay wall and jumped into the Abbey River. Her husband ran to the watchman to get him to assist but before Ryan had a chance to move John Lyddy ran to the spot where his wife had thrown herself in and jumped in after her. Ryan ran to the John Street station to get the assistance of Constables Bell and Clancy but when they returned to the scene of the incident there was no sight of either bodies.

It was later discovered that earlier that evening the couple had been drinking in a bar off Broad Street. There was some controversy about why the couple may have been arguing, but one interview revealed that one of their children was burned in an accident on the previous Monday evening when John was supposedly minding him. Whether that was the reason for the disagreement or not will never be known. During interviews and investigations it was disclosed that this had been the third, and ultimately final, time Sarah attempted to drown herself as she would sometimes, 'get a boiling passion if her husband spoke hastily to her.'

After the Lyddys family were informed of the accident, John's two brothers began dragging the river with nets in an attempt to recover the bodies. Sarah was found on 3 February 1897, about 14 miles from the city. She was laid to rest in Mount Saint Lawrence Cemetery. John's body was recovered a few days later, on 7 February, by Mount Kenneth just off the Dock Road in Limerick. His funeral was attended by members of the St Mary's Fife and Drum Band, of which he had been a member.

The newly orphaned children, all under the age of five, went to live with their grandparents, Matthew and Margaret Russell, in the Pennywell area of Limerick.

PUBLIC RANTING

Breaking up was so very hard to do, even in 1842. Life seemed to not be going well for Gerald Adams, who placed the following advert in the local newspapers warning the public against his estranged wife:

> I caution the public not to credit my wife Mary Adams after Quirk, as I am determined not to pay any debts she may contract after this. She having contrary to my wishes and to all remonstrance's left my house, and took with her all articles of furniture and beds which she claimed to be hers, and otherwise acted very improperly. Gerald Adams, Cornwallis Street – 5 Jan 1842.

CHALKING AND RIOTS

If you thought finding your love and then losing them was bad luck in Limerick, you might be surprised to hear that not even having a love in the first place could also bring strife to your life. There was a tradition in nineteenth-century Ireland known as 'Chalk Sunday', which derives its name from the old custom of children putting chalk marks upon bachelors and spinsters on the first Sunday of Lent.

Chalking Sunday of 1879 landed on 2 March. On that night there were two incidences of chalking that caused enough uproar to be noted in the local newspapers. Firstly on Mungret Street at about 7 p.m. a group of youths amused themselves by chalking everyone who passed, until one of the chalkees took enough offense and struck a chalker. Soon stones were flying in every direction and a number of youngsters had to be admitted to Barringtons Hospital with minor wounds.

The second incident was a much more violent affair. It took place in Clampett's Bow later that same evening. Clampett's Bow was a lane off John Street named after Isaac Clampett and was so narrow that it was difficult for two men to pass in it. This second row was sparked by the random chalking of passers-by but the culprits had long-standing grievances with each other. The four families involved were Connors, Halloran, Moran, and Meehan, who took the opportunity of a night of revelry to iron out their feud with sledgehammers and iron bars. This riot would have remained but a footnote in Limerick history if it were not for Thomas Stanley Tracey, who celebrated the siege in his poem 'The Battle of Clampett's Bow'.

LOST LIMERICK LOVE

Even world-renowned romantic novelist Jane Austen lost her heart in Limerick to a man, Tom Lefroy, during the Christmas of 1795. Both just barely twenty, met, talked, laughed and danced. This might not sound very racy in our modern world, but at the time this act caused Jane to receive a very stern letter from her sister, Cassandra, to which Jane responded: 'I am almost afraid to tell you how my Irish friend and I behaved'.

In letters to and from Jane over the following three years it is evident that she clung to the idea that herself and Tom would eventually marry. It was in November of 1798 that Jane found out about Tom's engagement to Mary Paul in Ireland and poor romantic Jane had her hopes dashed. Jane Austen pined after her lost Limerick love for the rest of her life and never married.

BETTER TO BE RICH THAN IN LOVE

The tale of Eileen Hinchey is a sad one indeed, as a young woman she went to work as a nursemaid in South Hill House in the 1860s. South Hill House was the home of Peter Tait, the clothing factory entrepreneur, and his brother John Tait, a troublemaker. During her time working at South Hill House Ellen became intimate with John and a child was conceived during the resulting affair. As Peter Tait was a highly respected member of Limerick's Society the usual recourse for a woman pregnant out of wedlock, being sent to the Good Shepherd Convent to atone for her sins, was avoided. Peter Tait sent both Ellen and the child to London. The child was placed in a Roman Catholic institution and Ellen was allowed to visit. However, Ellen tried the patience of the Mother Superior of the institution so much that she returned the child to the mother.

Next she was sent to New York and a sum of money given to the Roman Catholic Bishop to keep her. However, while there her conduct was apparently so scandalous that the bishop returned the money to her to be rid of her. She then returned to Limerick only to have her child removed from her as there were claims that she had attempted to murder the infant in London.

She was apprehended while in Limerick and, owing to the claims of attempted murder, she was certified insane by Dr Gelston and Dr Fitzgerald and removed from polite society in 1868 and placed in the lunatic asylum. What of John Tait? He simply walked away and was seldom heard from again in Limerick. He passed away in 1880.

LIMERICK PROSTITUTES OF THE PAST

History shows that Limerick's residents loved 'ladies of the night'. Between 1774 and 1794 in the Limerick House of Industry there were a total of fifty-eight harlots, nine whores and one strumpet.

A LOST WOMAN
MARY KELLY
IN MILLER'S COURT

On 19 June 1880 it was reported in the local press that a street walker who had been repeatedly convicted was sent to gaol (jail) for a month with a judgement for being, 'a common prostitute, night walker and drunkard'. With her being so young, approximately sixteen years old, she was also convicted of being 'a hag in vice'.

While on the subject of Limerick prostitutes, one must mention Mary Jane Kelly. She was a Limerick-born prostitute, born in 1863, and was also known as 'Marie Jeanette Kelly', 'Fair Emma', 'Ginger' or 'Black Mary'. It is widely believed that she was the fifth and final victim of the notoriously unidentified Jack the Ripper on 9 November 1888. She was described as 'quite attractive' and 'a pretty, buxom girl' who 'always wore a clean white apron but never a hat'.

10

THE
DOCTOR

Religion and science have had a long and tumultuous history of misunderstanding and strife; and Limerick was not immune to this lengthy battle. At the turn of the last century, Limerick was a city immersed in religion. With a population of over 30,000 souls, a mere 3,000 were not Roman Catholic. This vast congregation of churchgoers made up a great many parishes, convents, monasteries and missions located around the city.

It was into this staunch society that Dr Joseph John Long was asked to found the first Limerick branch of the Irish Church Mission to Roman Catholics in November of 1897. This mission was a branch of Evangelicalism which had been established in Dublin many years before. Their main objective was to offer medical help to the poor Irish Catholic people, while at the same time spreading the teachings of the Evangelical Church.

The then thirty-one-year-old doctor immediately moved to Limerick wife Ellen Jane, who was at the time expecting their third child, their two children, Ellen's mother and a number of servants. On arrival they began to set up house in Lansdowne Villas, on the Ennis Road. It was located just outside the heart of the city, over what was at the time known as Wellesley Bridge, but is today better known as Sarsfield Bridge.

As Dr Long was settling into his new family home and learning his way around Limerick he began making

observations of the people and the place he now found himself in. He is quoted as saying the people of Limerick were 'naturally good-natured and religious; they are easily led, and are still very much at the mercy of their priests, whom they regard as possessing supernatural powers.' It would unfortunately not take very long for the good doctor to realise just how much sway the local priests held in the city, especially regarding the compliance of the citizens.

Once the doctor and his family settled into their new home he began his search to find a suitable location for the Irish Church Mission of Limerick. Ideally, he wanted to find a building which was centrally located to provide the best service to those he intended to serve. This task proved to be very difficult for the doctor, who, with his non-Catholic vision, was not overly welcomed to the area.

Fortunately though the cleric and parishioners of the Episcopal Trinity Church on Catherine Street believed in the mission and offered moral support to the doctor when he needed it. The Trinity Church itself had been set up to aid the spiritual redemption of the blind women who were housed next door on Catherine Street.

After six weeks of searching to no avail, the doctor was about to give up when he spotted a group of painters in a premises on 46 Thomas Street. After obtaining the lease for the building, the doctor worked hard to transform it into a working dispensary. He was so absorbed in his duty that he never suspected the general public had any negative feeling towards him or his mission and the doors finally opened on 1 February 1898. Yet all the while the neighbours on Thomas Street were growing worried that the doctor was going to open a hospital or lunatic asylum, which they feared would lower the rents in the area.

Regardless of the mounting rumours and neighbourhood fears, after the mission opened it soon found its stride and in the first month they had 67 registered patients, which quickly rose to 441 in their second month. To assist with the ever-increasing number of patients, two new members of staff were added: Miss Condon in the dispensary and Nurse Shortle, who helped both in the mission itself as well as conducting home visits to those in need.

As time went on, things appeared to be going very well in the mission. Dr Long was sharing his medical knowledge with the sick and needy while simultaneously delivering 'The good word' to them. Each month up to September of that year the mission had over 500 attendees. It was during September that Dr Long began to wonder why the local Roman Catholic priests were so willingly letting their flock go to the mission and listen to the teachings of the Gospel of Jesus Christ.

His questions, and indeed suspicions, were soon answered. One day, as he cycled through the city, he heard a cry of 'Ha, Long!' from a rooftop. Ignoring it, he continued on his path and just a little further along a stone was thrown in his direction. He must have found the events curious and odd, but he most likely put it down to the heckling nature of miscreants and he eventually made it home that evening without further assault.

The next morning, Saturday 24 September 1898, just as the waiting room was filling up with about twenty patients, a great and powerful storm came bursting through the doors in the shape of Father Tierney from the St Alphonsus Redemptorist Church. The father loudly called out, 'This is a Souper's house – all Catholics must leave!'

At the time, a Souper was someone who would provide food to the hungry in return for a change of their religious allegiance. This terrified some of the shocked patients into

leaving the mission, which in turn caused Dr Long to shut the doors. This did nothing to sooth the righteous anger of Father Tierney, who continued to kick and shout from the outside. Father Tierney addressed the crowd that had begun to gather and continued his ravings: 'This is a Souper's house. The doctor is a Souper doctor. No Catholic is to go in there!'

The tale of this episode spread like wildfire through the city. The same evening another priest, Father Cregan, released a letter in the *Munster News* warning the public against the mission and against the doctor, who in his opinion was using the 'noble profession to which he belongs as the agent of a society that has for its object the perversion of Irish Catholics'.

In no time at all, in fact the very next day Dr Long was denounced from all the Roman Catholic Chapels in Limerick. The threats from the public became so vicious that the doctor feared for his safety and had to be put under police protection.

On the following Monday, Father Tierney reportedly preached to a large gathering of the Men's Confraternity and informed them 'to shun Dr Long as they would some contagious disease, and to avoid his moral medicine as they would poison'. The day after the father's announcement to the Confraternity, a priest rode up and down in front of the dispensary with a dog-whip in his hand in an effort to intimidate anyone who dared to come close or enter the 'proselytising swamp'.

Meanwhile, Bishop O'Dwyer of St Mary's Church made it a 'reserved sin' for any Catholic to attend the mission. This sin would be one in which only the bishop could absolve. Pretty much every step that Dr Long and his guards took in the city during the following days were met with heckles, shouts and assaults from stones being thrown.

That Friday a belligerent crowd of several hundred protested outside the dispensary on Thomas Street, shouting in time to a well-known tune of the day, 'We'll hang Dr Long on a sour apple tree'. A small riot erupted in which stones were thrown and before the crowd eventually dispersed several panes of glass were broken.

Throughout this chaos, and despite the warnings from the priests, many patients continued to visit the mission and avail of Dr Long's medical services, including a young woman who had recently returned from America to aid her dying mother. This young woman cared more about bringing her mother relief from her pain than she did the fear of trouble from her neighbours and called into the doctor for help. Unfortunately for her and her family, that very evening the woman's little cottage was attacked by a mob of angry locals. Not only was the door battered with sticks and stones, but the window was smashed as well. There was so much flying debris from the assault that the woman found it difficult to protect her mother and both ended up worse for wear.

Over the next few weeks a close eye was kept on the dispensary by members of the Confraternity, with men marching back and forth in front of the building during its opening hours. To the annoyance of Father Tierney, this did not deter all of the doctor's patients from entering to seek medical attention. As a result, at the father's next sermon he issued forth a decree onto the Confraternity that anyone who goes into that house of sin 'deserves no kind of patience at all, and they must be made to feel it'. He commanded the men to follow the patients to their homes where they should inform any and all neighbours as to the errors of their way. These acts pitted neighbour against neighbour and must have caused city-wide panic.

This continuous and unjust system of intimidation advocated and encouraged by Father Tierney robbed the people of Limerick the liberty to choose their own doctor and their own religion. As a result there were many beatings that took place because of visits to the dispensary. There were reported incidents of an old man who had his medicine smashed into the ground and a woman who was beaten with the handle of an umbrella by a priest because Dr Long had visited her sick children, after which she pleaded with the doctor not to return for fear of more retaliation.

That winter was harsh and bitterly cold, causing the watch of the Confraternity men to slow down. Consequently the visitors to the dispensary began to pick up again. Dr Long and the staff of the Mission gratefully took the patients in and did everything they could to relieve them of their ailments, but none gave in to the hope that the retribution of the Catholic Church was over. Of course it wasn't. In January, Father Tierney heard the tale of a young girl who had visited the dispensary and had 'lost her way'. Rumour had it she now knew her Saviour and proudly carried her Bible with her and asserted that she no longer had need for the Catholic Church, after which the father renewed his atrocious attack plans.

So the protests, attacks and general disapproval of the mission continued into the New Year, 1899. It truly seemed that Father Tierney had won his battle and that the only option for the doctor and the mission was to close the dispensary, pack up and return to Dublin with his family. Sometime in the year Nurse Shortle left the mission, but she was soon replaced by Nurse Dorothea Newton, who was profoundly amiable and quickly found her way into the hearts of the patients. With her arrival as a new member of staff the controversy at the dispensary calmed down and the number of patients began increasing once again.

Nurse Newton went on to open a Sunday school, which had about twelve regular attendees. The school operated successfully for a number of months until word spread throughout the community. Apparently some people were not happy about this and 'rough boys' began watching the children on the street and intimidated them in order to prevent them from attending. Furthermore, this Sunday school was to become the catalyst for the next round of commotion involving Father Tierney.

In an effort to maintain the sociability among the Sunday school attendees as well as their friends and neighbours, Nurse Newton planned a tea party for 4 January 1901 at 6.30 p.m. At 1 p.m. that day one of the children went to see Nurse Newton and informed her that Father Tierney had visited their house that morning and forbid anyone from attending the tea party. Through this child, Father Tierney sent the following message, 'If I ever meet her [Nurse Newton] on George Street [O'Connell Street], I would pull that hat off her head, and if I found her in that lane again I would kill her.' While she could not have been happy to hear of this interference, and certainly concerned about the threats made to her, she continued getting things prepared for the party.

The lane that the father referred to in his threat was a lane that a number of poor people who attended the mission lived, as well as the children who were to be present at the tea party. Despite the clamour and proposed menace, the nurse went to the lane and was greeted by much excitement over what the father had said, as well as the threats he made to the children and the nurse herself. This did nothing to prevent Nurse Newton from collecting the children at 6 p.m. from their parents' houses.

Regrettably, as the group made their way back to the mission along Catherine Street they were met by two priests, Father Tierney and Father Cregan. Father Tierney accosted them and said, 'These are all Catholic children, begone home out of that!' All but the youngest child, who held Nurse Newton's hand, scattered like the wind. Father Tierney ended up tearing the child out of the nurse's hand and tossing him in the gutter. Afterward he grabbed the nurse by both arms, shook her and threw her against the railings shouting, 'Why do you not go to Belfast and look after your own children who want looking after?' At that he let her go, turned around and left, but not before issuing yet another threat on her life.

Leaving Nurse Newton stunned and abashed on Catherine Street, the two priests went on to burst into the home of one of the children's mother who was home alone with her two-day-old infant. They continued to scold her for allowing her children to go to the mission and the Sunday school.

As soon as Dr Long was made aware of the situation, he arrived at the scene and asked the priests to leave as they were not called for or required at the present time. In response, the priests asked why he remained in a country where he was not wanted when there were millions of godless children in England. The doctor countered that, as an Irishman, he had no intention of leaving. The priests turned to the bedbound woman once more and compelled her to make the choice in that very moment between her priest and her doctor. The woman was frightened and made no reply. Eventually everyone went on their way and while the tea party went ahead, it had a greatly reduced turn out.

The Monday following this debacle, Father Tierney was back in front of the Confraternity, which had over 7,000 members at the time, once again preaching his message of indignation towards the doctor, the mission and the Sunday school. In the following days the mobs were back on the streets and several gentlemen were attacked after being mistakenly identified as Dr Long. One incident involved a Protestant clergyman who had to seek refuge in the convent on Clare Street to avoid the wrath of a mob of angry women. Due to malicious rumours spreading around the city, these women were under the false impression that Dr Long had gone into the very same convent and had not only 'stolen a young girl' but had also tore 'The veil from the Revd Mother, and spat in her face'.

Pandemonium ensued and, once again, Dr Long required a guard by his side just to walk down the street. Record has it that the few times Dr Long could be seen being escorted along the streets of Limerick city, he was bombarded with the old rhyme of 'We'll hang Dr Long on a sour apple tree' and 'Dr Long's mother keeps a soup shop in hell.' The impassioned mob event went so far as dressing up effigies of the doctor and burning them in the streets.

A few days later, on Friday evening, 18 January 1901, the doctor went to visit a friend and while inside with his police escort an assemblage gathered outside. Fearing the worse, the policeman suggested that Dr Long escape out of the back of the house, but the doctor would not abide this treatment any longer. He boldly walked out of the front door, where he was at once and without hesitation attacked with volleys of stones and mud. This continued until a young woman with a small child in her arms, who had once attended the dispensary, stood up beside him, knowing that the rioting crowd would not hurl the projectiles at the child. This act of courage by the woman kept the doctor safe until he reached George's Street, where he was once again set upon. The attacks had grown so vicious that as the doctor crossed Wellesley Bridge (Sarsfield Bridge) a group of the local police moved into formation in order to draw a cordon, preventing the crowd from pursuing the doctor any further.

Father Tierney's influence eventually reached the leaders of other parishes and on Sunday 27 January Father O'Donnell addressed St Michael's Temperance Association with a message. He assured his congregation that the recent troubles were not the fault of the Catholics but of those trying to convert the poor and suffering of the city to 'sell their birthright for a mess of pottage.' The *Limerick Chronicle* reported after that, 'Bigotry, so far as the Catholic masses are concerned, has never existed.'

The aggression that Dr Long and his family faced continued, but he would not be swayed from his mission, or his life. Along with the aggression, many rumours were spread about the doctor and what he was really doing in the city, which had already endangered more than one citizen. One Saturday, 9 February 1901, the doctor and Mrs Long, accompanied by their personal police escort, went to visit a friend at the Protestant Orphan Home on Henry Street.

After being seen at this location, another rumour began to circulate that the doctor had actually brought a Roman Catholic girl to the orphanage and it filled many locals with rage and disgust. As a result, an agitated mob gathered and greeted the doctor and his party with booing, groaning and shouting as they left the building. As the Longs made their way home, they were covered in flour, which was dropped on them from above from windows as they passed. Once again the police cordons were formed on the bridge to prevent the mob from following them home.

Following the weekend's altercations, a number of arrests were made and Dr Long was called to the court, not to act as a witness but instead to be cross-examined by the bench. Mr Hickey, a Protestant magistrate, strongly condemned the Mission. He stated before the court that he was a very involved and accomplished Protestant, and that he had never once heard of the branch of Evangelicalism that the doctor came to Limerick to spout. The implications by Mr Hickey made it seem that the doctor truly was in Limerick to cause dissent and disorder to not only the local Roman Catholic order, but to true Protestants as well.

It didn't take long for the court to dismiss the cases against those arrested for violent acts against the doctor and his family. The blame for all the fracas was laid solely Dr Long's door. The judges final statement included a proclamation that those who had paid Dr Long to be in Limerick should make haste in taking the required steps to have him removed from the city immediately. This decision was met with considerable applause from the attending audience.

Following this judgement the streets were engulfed with posters headed 'Long Must Go!' The *Munster News* and the *Limerick Echo* also joined the chorus, spreading word of the courts manifesto that Dr Long must be made to leave Limerick.

By 28 February 1901 the police authorities had become so anxious about the safety of the Long family that the County Inspector of the RIC wrote to the mission leaders in

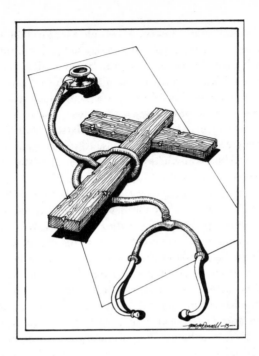

Dublin suggesting that the only way to ensure the security of the doctor was to restrict his movements in the city.

It was reported that upon a visit from the Roman Catholic Lord Chief Justice of Ireland, who was visiting Limerick for the Assize, he had called for the people of Limerick to just pass the doctor and his mission by, that they should not make a martyr of him. He even went so far as to say that the 'respectable Protestant community' should also not associate with the Irish Church Mission in any way, shape or form.

One of the final major incidents came in June of 1901, when, after visiting a Protestant patient, Hugh McCabe in Thomondgate, the doctor was accosted by Revd Edmond O'Leary, parish priest of St Munchin's, who threatened his life were he to continue to stay and conduct his work in Limerick. The doctor initiated immediate legal proceedings against the Revd O'Leary. Although Margaret McGrath and Margaret Casey were arrested, charged and fined for assaulting the doctor by throwing bricks and eggs at him during the incident with Revd O'Leary, his case was still dismissed after the Lord Chief Justice's previous statements were reiterated about the doctor and his mission.

These cases eventually led to a debate in Parliament, where there was uproar in response to the treatment of the doctor and his family, as well as the mission, its staff and its patients in Limerick.

In an effort to ease the turbulence in the city the doctor and his family decided to close the dispensary and leave Limerick for a month. Upon their return the Long family were refused lifts on all jarveys, or taxi carriages, in the city, resulting in their movement around the city being by foot or not at all. Dr Long was given no reprieve from the treatment he had grown accustomed to and it couldn't have surprised him when the Mayor of Limerick took a case against the doctor for causing a public disturbance while he tried to procure a lift in a jarvey for himself and his family on 10 August 1901 at the cross roads at George Street (O'Connell Street) and William Street. This case was also dismissed.

Father Tierney left Limerick 5 May 1902 but it did not stop the threats or abuse towards the doctor, though it did lessen to a more tolerable level. While Father Creagh, who took up the job as the leader of the Arch-Confactionary, was just as tolerant as his predecessor, his sights were set on the Jewish Community in Limerick rather than that of the Protestant one – leading to the well-known attack on the Limerick Jewish Community in 1904.

As the doctor had a passion for his mission he would remain in Limerick for many years to come. Though the actions of his first few years would cause him to move further out of the limelight while continuing to help the poor and needy of Limerick.

11

TRAINS, CARTS
AND JARVEY CARS

HORSES

Trundling Hoops and Horses
In 1838 Limerick, the game of 'trundling hoops' consisted
of a large metal wheel, typically off of a beer barrel and a
large stick of some sort. The game was played by standing
the wheel upright, putting it in motion down a path and

keeping it rolling along with thrusts from the stick. While fun for the young people who found delight in the sport, the horses that were transporting citizens to and fro did not find it very enjoyable. The sounds of the metal clanking, thrusting movements of the arms and sticks, and the wheels suddenly flying past would often frighten the horses and cause accidents, both minor and major. As a result, the mayor, Garrett Hugh Fitzgerald, issued a warning to the residents of the area against playing this game on the footpaths and in the streets of the city. In his declaration he included his concern for the horses and the havoc that was caused when they became startled. To help enforce this warning, Mayor Fitzgerald sent out a rider to the police to suppress this activity to the best of their ability. A rider was an official notification used to inform the police stations what has or is happening and to do what they can to stop the future occurrences of the specified activity.

Horses on the Loose

In February 1897 a horse got loose on Roches Street and somehow managed to get himself into a house. Not only

that, but he made it upstairs and into one of the apartments, shocking and probably scaring the life out of the occupants. With a considerable amount of difficulty, the horse was eventually brought out of the apartment, down the stairs and back onto the street. Due to the ruckus caused and the huge effort it took to retrieve the animal, there was a large crowd of expectant spectators waiting outside to watch the successful rescue.

In that same month another horse escaped his owner on Carey's Road, where the owner was unloading cushions from the accompanied cart. This time the horse, cart still in tow, managed to run all the way through the city until finally making his way across the river. He was finally caught near St Munchin's church and returned safely to its owner.

TRAINS

Death by Stampede
On Sunday, 12 July 1903, some 700 excursionists travelled to Limerick to attend the Gaelic Games at the Market Field. Those from Dublin were set to depart on the 8.15 p.m. train. At the Limerick Railway Terminus an immense crowd of almost a thousand people had gathered to see them off. The usual precaution of only allowing ticketholders onto the platform was strictly enforced by the station officials only allowing travellers through one side of the open gate and ushering them through in an orderly fashion. Without warning, the large crowd that had formed on the other side managed to open the other gate, causing a rush of people pushing their way through. Stephen Noone, who had worked as a platform inspector for about eight years, was hit by the wave of people who knocked him to the ground and proceeded to trample over him. It took a few moments to get the crowd under control and unfortunately by that stage Stephen Noone had been killed by the stampede.

Don't Skip School, Kids

On 30 September 1898 thirteen-year-old Joseph Smith rose as usual in his family home on Mungret Street at half-past eight in the morning and ate his breakfast with his family before heading off for the day. He gathered his books and set off for St John's Boys School. On his way he met his ten-year-old cousin, John Smith, who was on his way to a different school. The boys hatched a scheme and decided to skip school and spend the day together instead. They went to the railway bridge at the canal and proceeded to follow the track to the Singland Bridge before they were hit by the 10.15 train from Limerick to Ennis. A young child came upon the prostrate boys on the track and immediately went to a nearby house, where a woman alerted the authorities. Within moments the fire crews attended the scene and both boys were carried away, alive, on stretchers to Barrington's hospital. Sadly Joseph's injuries proved too severe and he passed away at seven minutes passed three that day. By contrast, John walked away with a slight head injury and a portion of his right boot torn away and went on to make a full recovery.

Train Amputation

At one o'clock on 13 April 1903, John McDonnell arrived home from the dentist, Joseph Vincent Coogan on Upper Mallow Street, where he was employed as a groom. After eating his meal he left for his cousin's house. At approximately 4 p.m. he met his wife and sister at the Limerick station to see his sister off to Dublin. She boarded the train and John took her hand through an open window while the train was moving off to wish her goodbye. At this precise moment he slipped between the couplings, released his sister's hand and became trapped under the train, which continued to move, and the last carriage passed over his legs. He was taken to Barrington's Hospital, where he arrived still conscious and sober. It was discovered that both of his legs had been completely crushed and the surgeon determined that they required amputation. The operation took place, and while both limbs were successfully removed, the trauma proved to be too much on John's shocked body and he died half an hour later. An inquest was held the following day and the usual verdict of an accidental death was reached. A rider was attached to the judgement recommending that the widow should receive consideration from the Railway Company. This rider was fulfilled a few months later when John's widow received £100 compensation from the railway company.

Unsafe Railway Bridge

Michael Moore was a watchman working for the Great Southern and Western Railway Company. On the night 13 July 1905 he was overseeing repairs to the railway bridge over the canal. The bridge had beams about 12 inches wide and the planks were between 2 and 5 feet apart. It would seem that Michael had missed his footing while going over these planks and fell between them, knocking his knee and ribs in the process. He fell into 6 feet of water and subsequently drowned. At the inquest it was decided that the bridge was, unsurprisingly, unsafe for workmen to pass over.

CARTS

A Barrel of Porter

At half past two on Saturday, 14 April 1900, on Sarsfield Street, twenty-one-year-old John McCarthy was standing on the rear of his cart in the process of loading a sack of flour when he lost his balance and slipped backwards. His fall caused the hind part of the cart to tilt downwards. John attempted to grasp a barrel of porter that was also on the cart to try to prevent his falling to the ground. Sadly, with the angle of the cart, it caused the barrel to come tumbling down after him as he fell flat on the ground. The iron band of the barrel struck him above the eye, crushing his skull. At the inquest, it was believed that although the cart was the most common form of cart used by the countrymen of the time, it was not of a sufficient quality to transport barrels of porter.

Spooked Horses and Flying Fruit

Kate Woods, a fifty-five-year-old fruit seller from the Clare/Pennywell area, was walking across Matthew Bridge in the city with her goods on 9 January 1902. A horse and cart was travelling in her direction when a gust of wind picked up a newspaper from the ground. This newspaper flew in front of the horse, spooking it and caused it to bolt. The horse ran straight into Kate Woods, knocking her to the ground, sending her fruit flying through the air, and killing her instantly.

BOATS

Flyboats

The lack of a local railway service created a demand for a passenger boat service along the canal to connect with the railway network. These were called 'flyboats', which were long narrow boats with covered seating for passengers. They were usually towed by two horses, often galloping, along the towpath beside the river using a harness and rope. Travelling this way was much faster than any other boats on the canal at the time. Flyboats were granted 'right of way' over other boats, which had to release their towlines to let them pass. They could also go to the front if there was a queue of boats at lock gates. The flyboat service on this and on other canals provided a cheaper alternative to travelling by stage-coach, which could be very uncomfortable on bad roads.

The route which these flyboats took began at Lock Quay and travelled along the canal to Troy's Lock, where once stood Harrold's Hotel and the Troy's Lock Keepers house, neither of which remain today. Harrold's Hotel, owned by Richard Harrold whose family built the St Patrick's Church,

was a fine establishment in its time, where the city's most prestigious residents and visitors stayed. After the hotel was abandoned and before it was demolished, it was considered to be haunted by local schoolchildren who would run past it, doing their best to not look in the gloomy windows.

Death at the Regatta

In 1897, the regatta, a popular boat show, was held close to Limerick City on Friday 16 July. Edward Pigott was hired by the Regatta Committee to ferry people up and down the Shannon on the steamer called the *Flying Huntsman*. This steamer was docked near the end of the regatta course at Mount Kennett and was due to leave for a race when a number of people boarded the gangway. Just as Mr Pigott decided that the steamer should set off and he was shutting the railings so no others were able to board, Mr William Cronin came running up to him.

As the *Flying Huntsman* was edging away from the gangway William Cronin insisted on boarding but Mr Pigott thought different and grabbed him about the waist in an effort to stop him. In the struggle both men fell over the railings of the gangway on to the pontoon, a platform of the boat outside the paddle box. Another man on board the boat ran to them and caught them both by the hands, but William Cronin slipped from his grasp and fell into the water between the steamer and the quay. In a matter of moments a rope was thrown but the man had already sunk under the water. It took less than five minutes to retrieve his lifeless body with grappling hooks from under the *Flying Huntsman*. It was decided at the inquest that no blame should be placed on Edward Pigott, whose defence was that he had only stopped the man in an attempt to carry out his duty on behalf of the Regatta Committee, who had insisted that all launch times must be adhered to strictly.

William Cronin's subsequent funeral took place from St Michael's Church to Mungret Cemetery. The funeral had a huge turnout, including family, friends and the general public of the community, as well as the mayor and several representatives from the local shipping firms, with a procession of over eighty vehicles.

Tragedy in the Water

Four boys called Thomas McCann, James Barnes, Bernard Matthews and his brother William took a small cot that had been lying in the Matthews brothers' yard for the prior two years to the riverbank near the corporation baths on 23 August 1898. Both sides and the bottom of the boat were made of timber and the top was covered with canvas. The boys amused themselves for a time pulling it in and out of the water when eventually James Barnes and Bernard Matthews decided to get aboard. However, the boat quickly began to fill with water so they jumped back ashore. They made a further two attempts to float the cot but it was not water-tight and on the third attempt it filled with water and regrettably sank.

Bernard Matthews then fell into the water; William went to the aid of his brother who could not swim. He caught Bernard by the collar of his shirt, but Bernard turned and grabbed hold of his brother about the neck and they both sank. James was also in the water by this stage and in some difficulty but another boy came to his rescue by pushing the upturned craft towards him, which he held onto so he could stay afloat. The Matthews brothers resurfaced but William was forced to release his grip on Bernard in order to save himself, on doing so his brother sank and subsequently drowned.

The Titanic

Everyone knows the story of the *Titanic*; whether it's from history taught at primary school or that movie where love can conquer all, even the icy seas. One way or another, 100 years later, the story is as poignant as it was the day the *Titanic* hit the ill-fated iceberg in the Atlantic Ocean. There were 2,242 people on board the ship, 1,513 of which that lost their lives that night, 8 of whom came from Limerick.

All of the Limerick victims of the *Titanic* disaster were third-class passengers who had boarded in Queenstown, Cork. Their fateful journey had begun on the morning of 11 April 1912, when scores of Irish immigrants attended their last Mass in Ireland in St Colman's Cathedral. They then made their way to the Deepwater Quay, where they boarded the tender *America* and were ferried out to the *Titanic*, which moored off Roches Point. For the following it would be their final journey:

Colbert, Patrick – Kilconlea, Abbeyfeale, Co. Limerick
Dooley, Patrick – Patrickswell, Co. Limerick
Foley, Joseph – Mountplummer, Broadford, Co. Limerick
Lane, Patrick – Limerick City, Co. Limerick
Moran, Daniel James – Askeaton, Co. Limerick
O'Brien, Thomas – Pallasgreen, Co. Limerick
Ryan, Patrick – Askeaton, Co. Limerick
Scanlan, James – Rathkeale, Co. Limerick

As can be seen above, all the Limerick victims were male, which is presumably a reflection on the women and children first priority that was put in place during the evacuation of the

ship as well as the fact that there were a lot more men on board than women and children. That said, one of the Limerick victims, Patrick Lane, was a mere sixteen years of age.

Patrick, a resident of Clare Street in Limerick City, was heading to New York City. He had been an assistant in a marine store in Limerick prior to his departure. One of his fellow Limerick passengers, Nellie O'Dwyer, was asked to keep an eye on him by his parents before he left. She survived but never forgave herself for losing him. Below is the record of Patrick Lane and his family from the 1911 census Clare Street:

Father: James Lane, 46, Labourer in Condensed Factory, can read and write.
Mother: Margaret, 38, Read and write, 19 years married, 8 children born, 6 children alive.
Children:
Bridget, 18, can read and write.
Patrick, 15 (died on Titanic), Assistant in Marine Store.
Michael, 12, Scholar.

Mary Kate, 10, Scholar.

Theresa, 4.

James, 1.

It is unknown whether any of these men's remains were recovered, but it's a sad fact that none of their bodies were ever identified. It undoubtedly took years for the families who lost their loved ones to rebuild their lives, and now, those whose lives were cut prematurely short in such a tragic way, have earned their place in history and should be remembered as the brothers, sons, uncles and friends that they were.

HOT-AIR BALLOONS

The eighteenth-century citizens of Limerick were quick to find new technologies and to use them in the city. On 21 November 1783 in Annonay, France the first untethered manned flight was performed in a hot-air balloon. Less than two years later a Limerick man would attempt to perform the same feat in Ireland.

On 27 April 1786, at half-past four in the evening, Richard Crosbie ascended from the House of Industry on Clancy Strand in a car affixed to an air balloon which he had invented in 1774. The winds were blowing south-east by east, and Crosbie travelled over the counties of Limerick, Kerry and Clare until, at ten past six, he landed in Ballygreen.

Richard Crosbie was born in 1755 in Co. Wicklow. He was a staggering 6 foot 3 inches tall with a fat, ruddy face. It was said that there was scarcely an art or trade of which he had not some practical knowledge. In late 1784 he exhibited his 'Aeronautic Chariot', his air balloon, made of wood and cloth, designed and built by himself. The citizens of Limerick were quick off the mark to help fund an attempt at flight from the city and created a committee for this event in December 1785. There were a few false starts, owing to lack of funding and bad

weather, before Crosbie could finally make his ascent. When he landed, the locals reportedly ran in fear, thinking him from space, but the next day, Saturday 2 May, they chaired him through the city in praise for his successful feat.

On 3 September 1848 a Mr Hampton, Mr Hampden Russell, and Mr Townsend also made a successful ascent in a hot-air balloon, *Erin-Go-Bragh*, from a yard in Cecil Street.

MOTOR BICYCLES AND MOTOR CARS

In 1904 motor cars and motorcycles were first registered in Limerick. Some of the first people to have cars and motorbikes were such notable names as James Bannatyne, James Ellis Goodbody, Thomas Goodbody, the Cleeve brothers from the Condensed Milk Company, Patrick Coonerty, Robert Moorehead and Thomas Shepherd, Captain of the King's Regiment.

Leabharlanna Poiblí Chathair Bhaile Átha Cliath
Dublin City Public Libraries